Authentic
GUITAR-TAB
Edition ™
Includes Complete Solos

LED ZEPPELIN

CLASSICS

D1571694

© 1993 WARNER BROS. PUBLICATIONS
Exclusive Print Rights Administered by ALFRED PUBLISHING CO., INC.
All Rights Reserved

Any duplication, adaptation or arrangement of the compositions
contained in this collection requires the written consent of the Publisher.
No part of this book may be photocopied or reproduced in any way without permission.
Unauthorized uses are an infringement of the U.S. Copyright Act and are punishable by Law.

CONTENTS

Key To Notation Symbols

Whole Lotta Love

Words and Music by
JIMMY PAGE, ROBERT PLANT,
JOHN PAUL JONES, JOHN BONHAM
and WILLIE DIXON

© 1969, 1990 SUPERHYPE PUBLISHING
All rights administered by WB MUSIC CORP.
All Rights Reserved

Fill 1

9

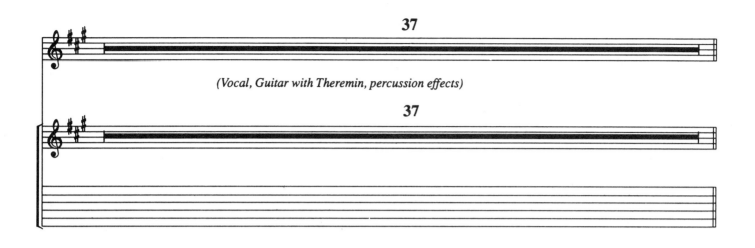

(Vocal, Guitar with Theremin, percussion effects)

Electric Guitar 2

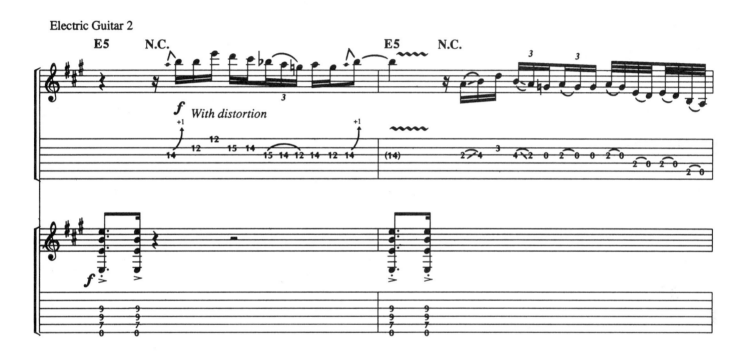

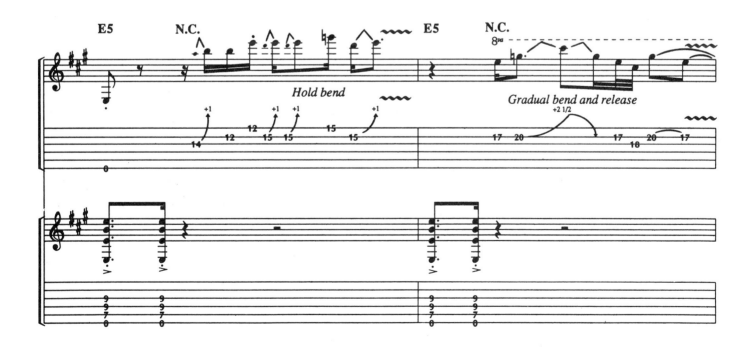

Ma,__ ma,__ ma,__ ma!__

Ma,__ ma,__ ma,__ ma!__ Whoa!__

Shake__ for me, girl. I wan-na be your back door man!

CELEBRATION DAY

Words and Music by
JIMMY PAGE, ROBERT PLANT
and JOHN PAUL JONES

Hard Rock and Soul, Brisk with swing ♩ = 120

Intro: **G7**

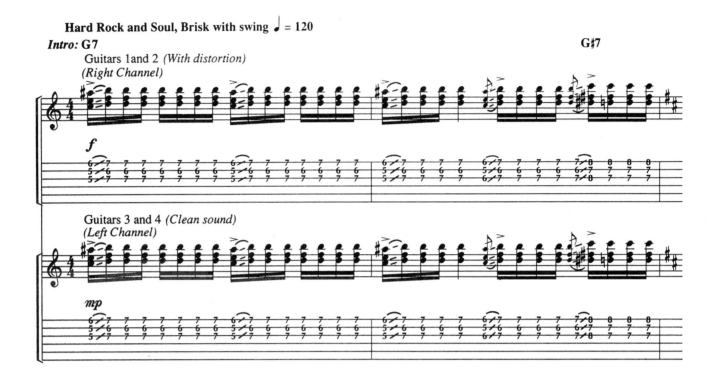

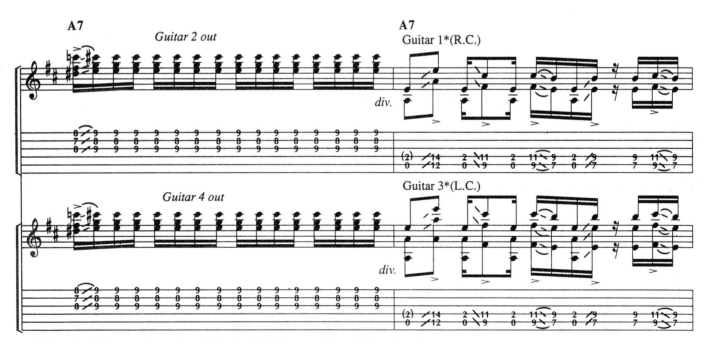

Guitar 1 with harmonizer effect (a Perfect fifth above) and/or additional tracks.
Guitar 3 with harmonizer effect (a Perfect fifth above and one octave below) and/or additional tracks.
These octaves are beyond the standard tuning register and are therefore omitted from the Tablature. The original part (without effects) is notated in downstems and parenthesis on the fifth string of the tablature. All harmony effects are quieter than the original sources driving them.

© 1970, 1991 SUPERHYPE PUBLISHING
All rights administered by WB MUSIC CORP.
All Rights Reserved

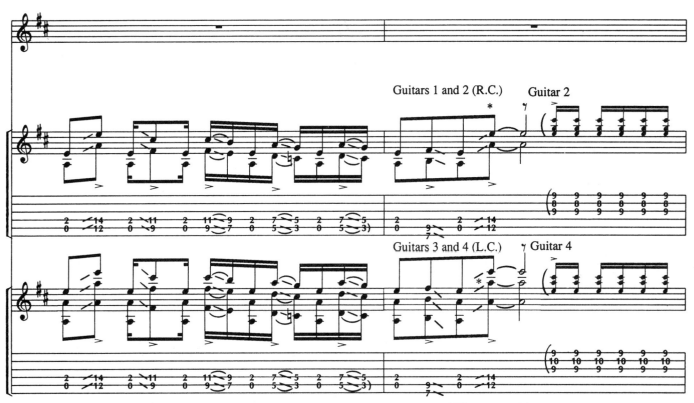

Guitars 1 and 2 (R.C.) Guitar 2

Guitars 3 and 4 (L.C.) Guitar 4

*The return of Guitars 2 and 4 (in parentheses).

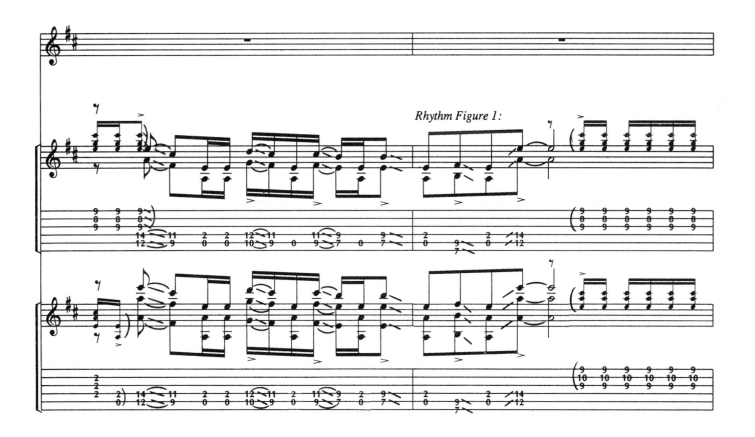

Rhythm Figure 1:

Verse 1:

A7

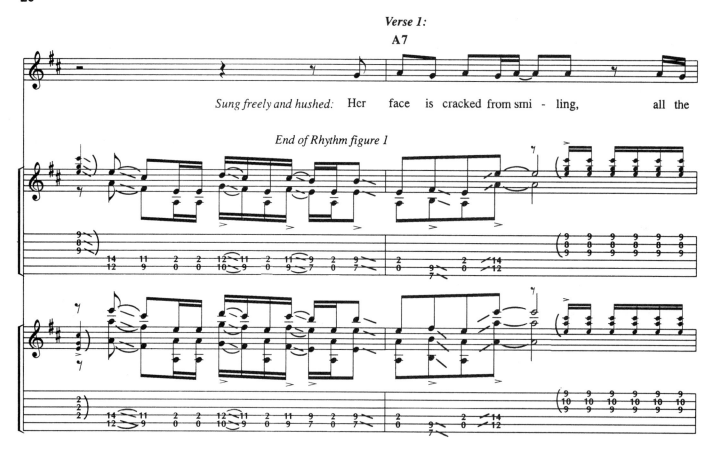

Sung freely and hushed: Her face is cracked from smi - ling, all the

End of Rhythm figure 1

fears that she's— been hid - ing and it seems that pret - ty

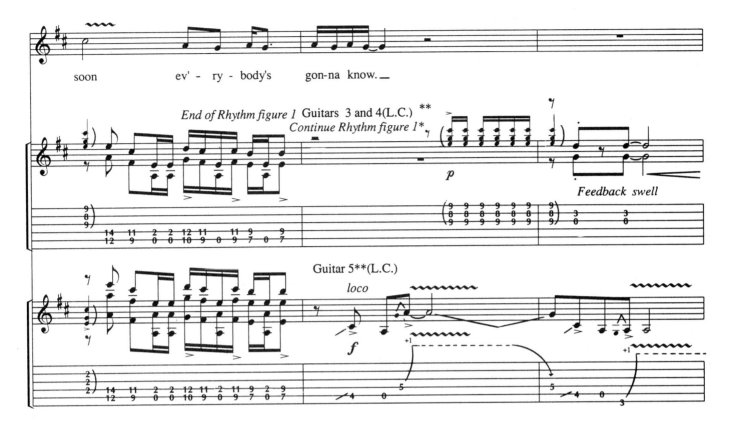

soon   ev' - ry - body's   gon-na know. __

*Guitars 1 and 2, right channel only with ad lib variations.
**Guitar 3 is upstemmed. Guitar 4: octave effect off, perfect fifth effect on.
***Rhythm figure 2.
****Les Paul, both pick-ups. Perfect fifth harmony one octave above is
      also audible here and throughout the song. Possibly a seperate track (8va) with harmonizer.

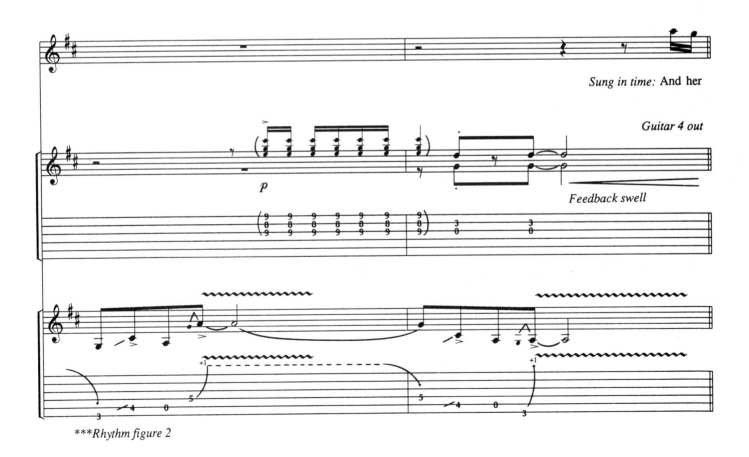

***Rhythm figure 2

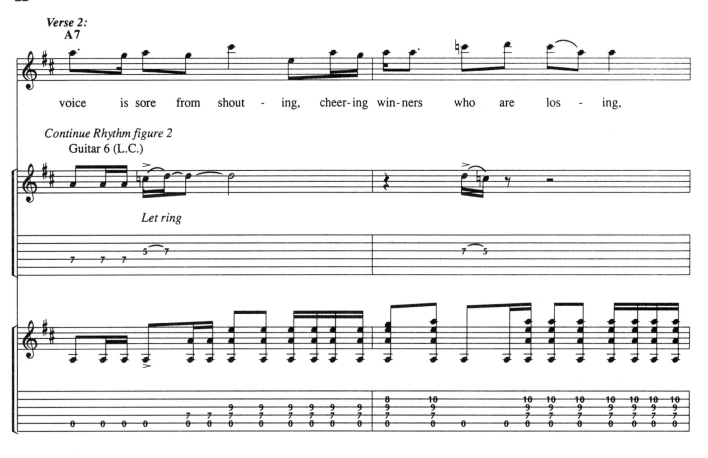

Verse 2:
A7

voice is sore from shout - ing, cheer-ing win-ners who are los - ing,

Continue Rhythm figure 2
Guitar 6 (L.C.)

Let ring

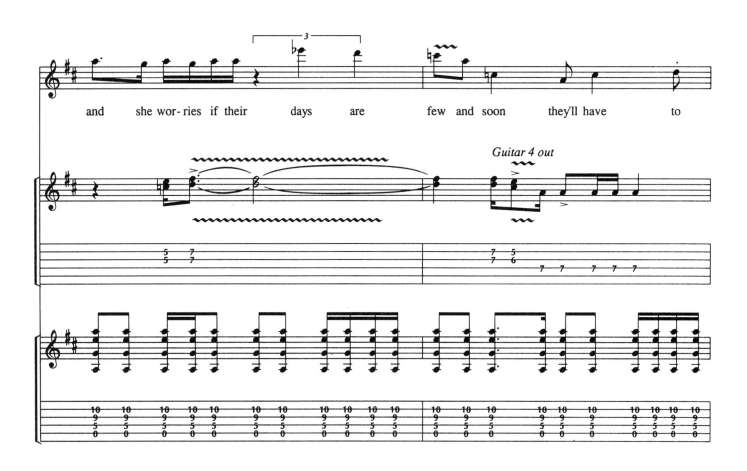

and she wor-ries if their days are few and soon they'll have to

Guitar 4 out

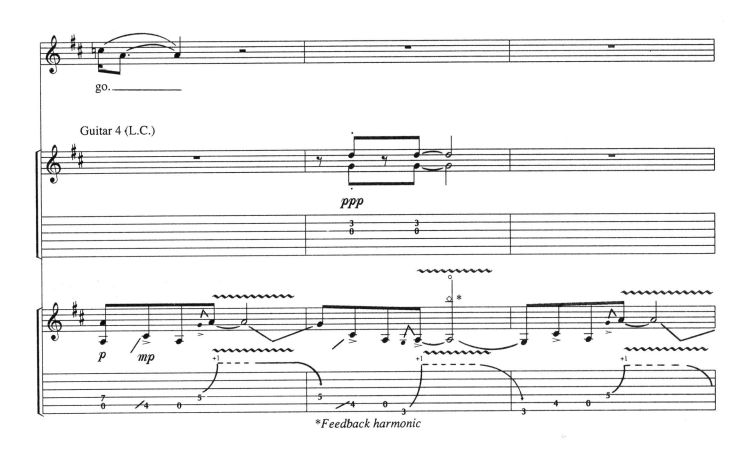

*Feedback harmonic

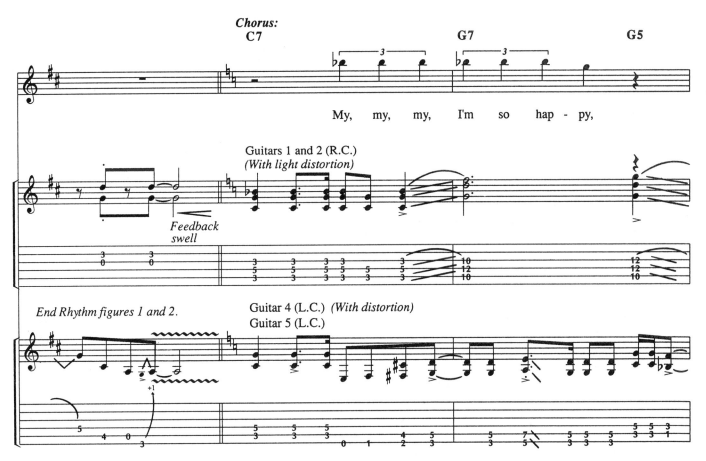

Chorus:
C7

My, my, my, I'm so hap - py,

Top note in chords barely audible. Clean sound on right channel, distortion on left.

Top note in chord barely audible. Clean sound on right channel, distortion on left.

*Verse 3: *

A7

She hears them talk of new ways_ to pro - tect the home_ she lives in,

Guitar 6 (L.C.)

Guitar 5 (L.C.)

Resume Rhythm figure 1 (Guitars 1 and 2, right channel only)
and Rhythm figure 2 (Left channel) with ad lib variations.

A7

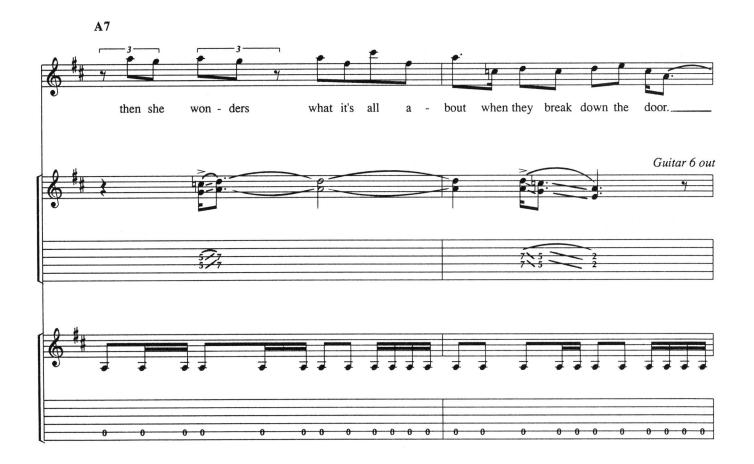

then she won - ders what it's all a - bout when they break down the door.____

Guitar 6 out

A7

Guitar 4 (L.C.)

pp

p   *mp*

Verse 4:
A7

Her name is Brown or White or Black,   you know ver-y   well,___   you

Guitar 4 out **Guitar 6 (L.C.)**

p

Feedback swell

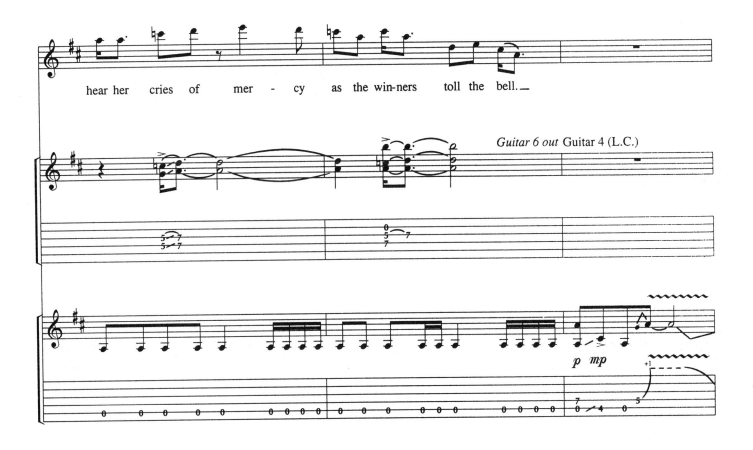

hear her cries of mer - cy as the win-ners toll the bell.

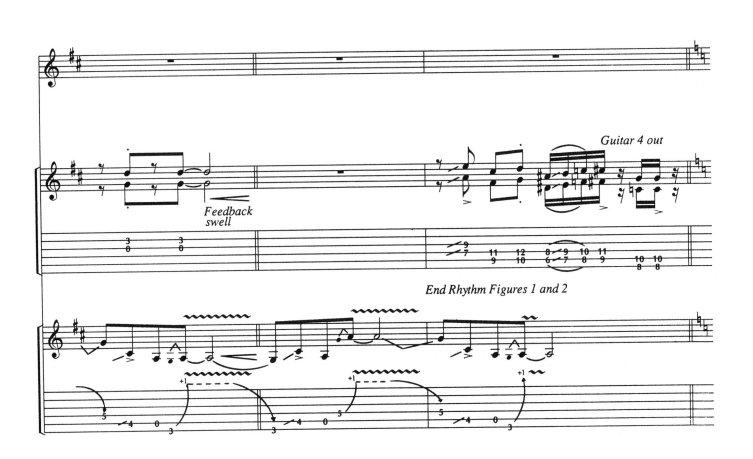

Chorus:

My, my, my I'm so_ hap - py, I'm gon-na join_ the band____ yeah._ We gon-na sing and dance in cel-e-bra - tion_

Slide into C5 from a whole step below during bridge solo.

We're   in the prom-ised   land.

Bridge: *Guitar solo with Rhythm figure 2.*

Resume Rhythm figure 1 Guitars 1 and 2, right channel only)
and Rhythm figure 2 (left channel) with ad lib variations, through the rest of the song.

but the price you pay to no - where has in- creased a dol-lar more. *Spoken: Yes it*

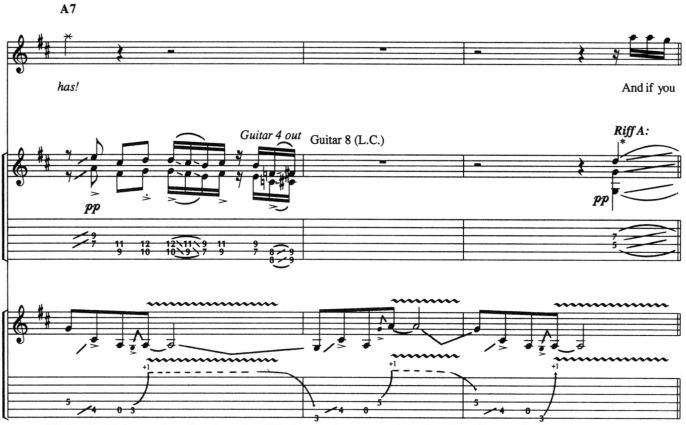

has!   And if you

*Guitar 8 with harmonizer effect (a perfect fifth above and one octave below) and/or other tracks.
The octaves are omitted from the tablature.
The original part (without effects) is notated in downstems and the lower line of tablature.*

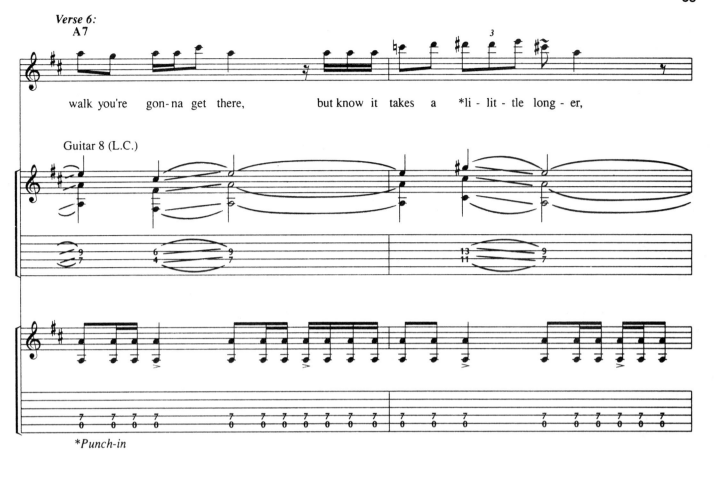

*Punch-in

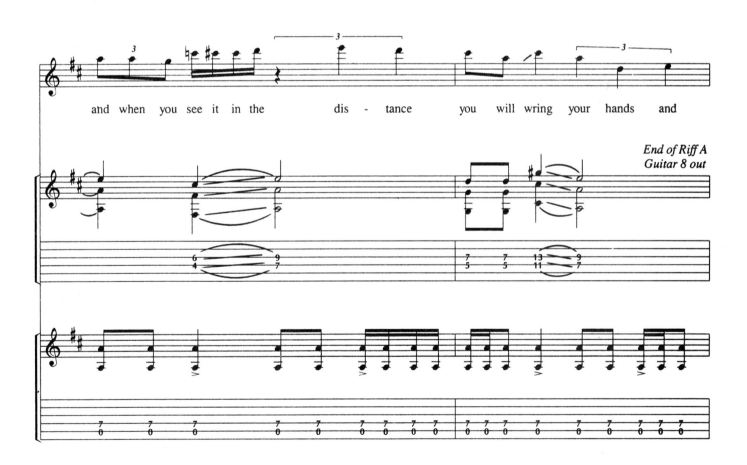

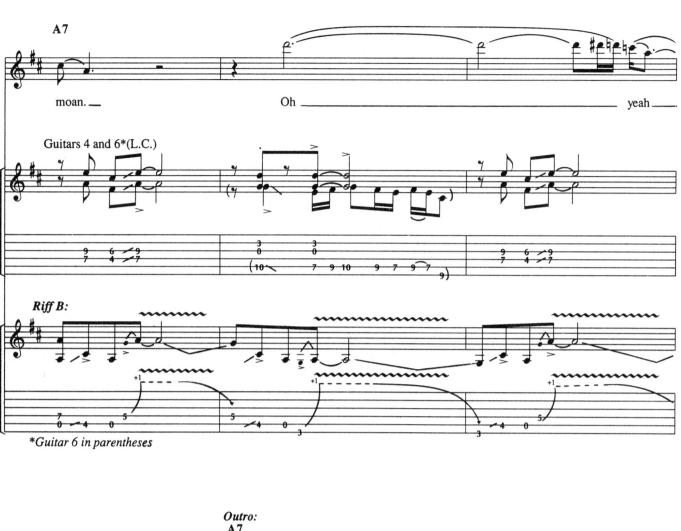

*Guitar 6 in parentheses

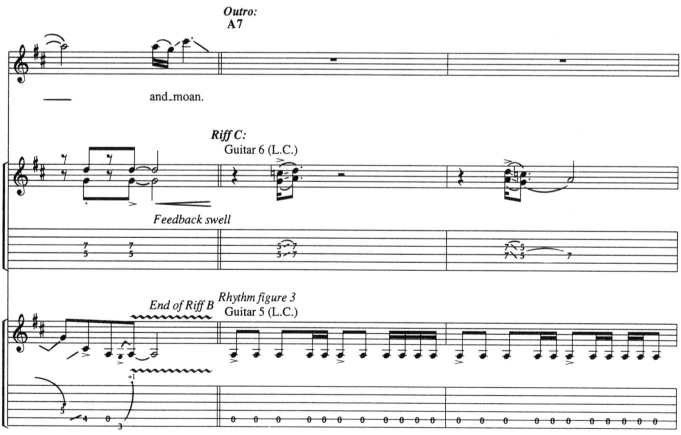

Ooh _____ yeah, ___ yeah, yeah,

End of Riff C

End of Rhythm fig. 3   *Guitar 5 out*

With Riff B
A7

yeah, yeah, ___   moan, ___   moan. _____   *Guitar 6 out*
Let ring

*Guitars 6 and 7

div.   *f*

Guitar 5: Left channel and Guitar 7: Right channel and notated in downstems.

Riff B out With Riffs A and C and Rhythm figure 3 with ad lib variations.

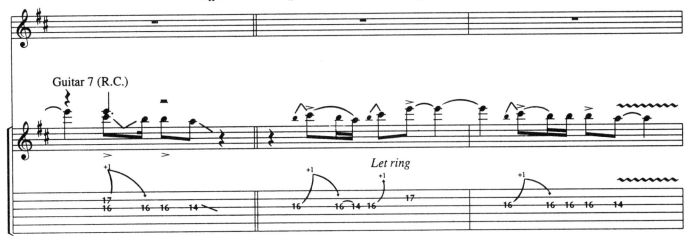

Guitar 7 (R.C.)

Let ring

*Guitar 7 panned from right to left to right channels over the next four measures.

Refrain of Verse 6:

bye, bye, yeah. ___

If you

Begin fade out

**Flanging effect on all left channel backing guitars over next three measures.

walk you're gon-na get there, but know it takes a lit-tle long-er, and when ya'

A7

Fade out

see it in the dis - tance you will wring your hands__ and moan. _____

*VSO (variable speed oscilater) effect on all left channel backing guitars through the fade out.

Ramble On

Words and Music by
JIMMY PAGE and
ROBERT PLANT

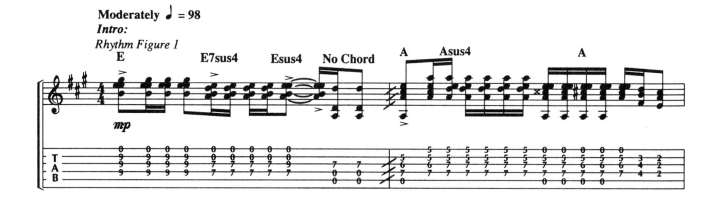

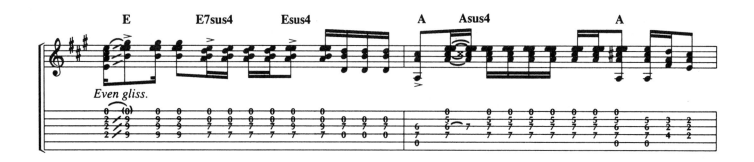

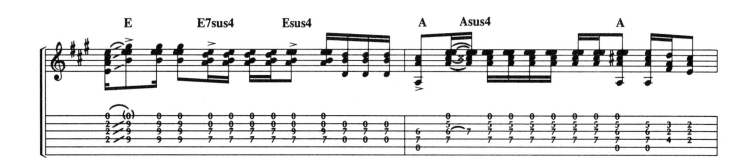

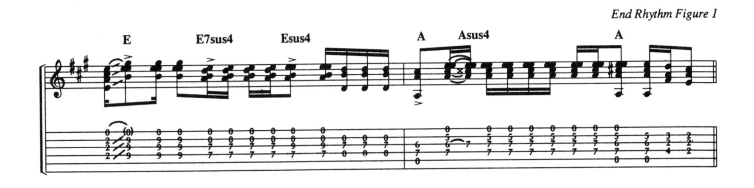

© 1969, 1990 SUPERHYPE PUBLISHING
All rights administered by WB MUSIC CORP.
All Rights Reserved

Verse 1: *With Rhythm Figure 1 (2 times)*

Leaves are fall - in' all a - round, (it's)

Features ad lib. variations of basic figure.
Chord symbols outline basic harmony.

time I was on my way.____

Even gliss.

Thanks to you I'm much o-bliged,

for such a plea-sant____ stay.____

43

End Rhythm Figure 1

Have _____ to ram-ble on _____

With Rhythm Figure 1

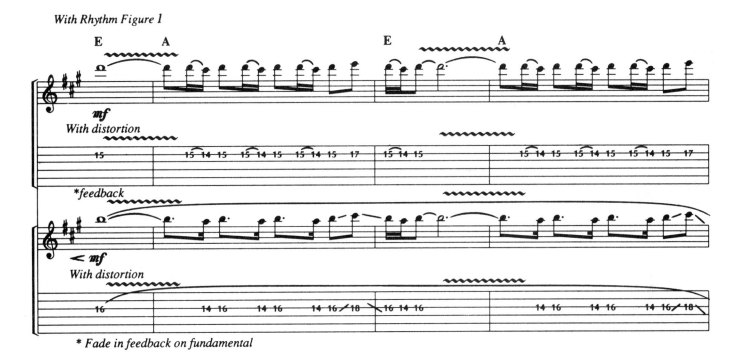

mf
With distortion

feedback

mf
With distortion

* *Fade in feedback on fundamental*

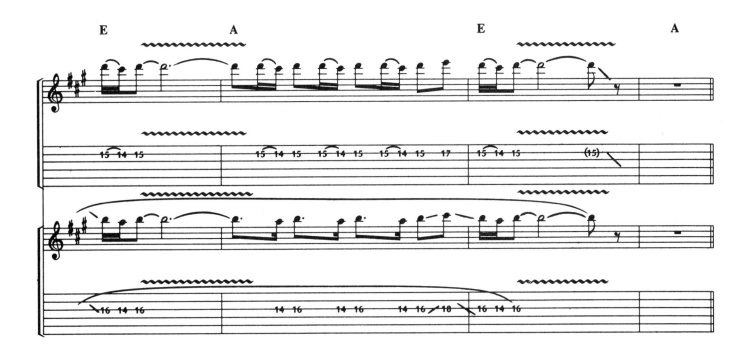

With Rhythm Figure 2 (4 times)

48

Interlude:

*Two Guitars notated with opposite stemming.
Downstems notated to right of / in TAB when necessary.

With Rhythm Fill 1

Rhythm Fill 1

Let arpeggio ring

Verse 3:
With Rhythm Figure 1

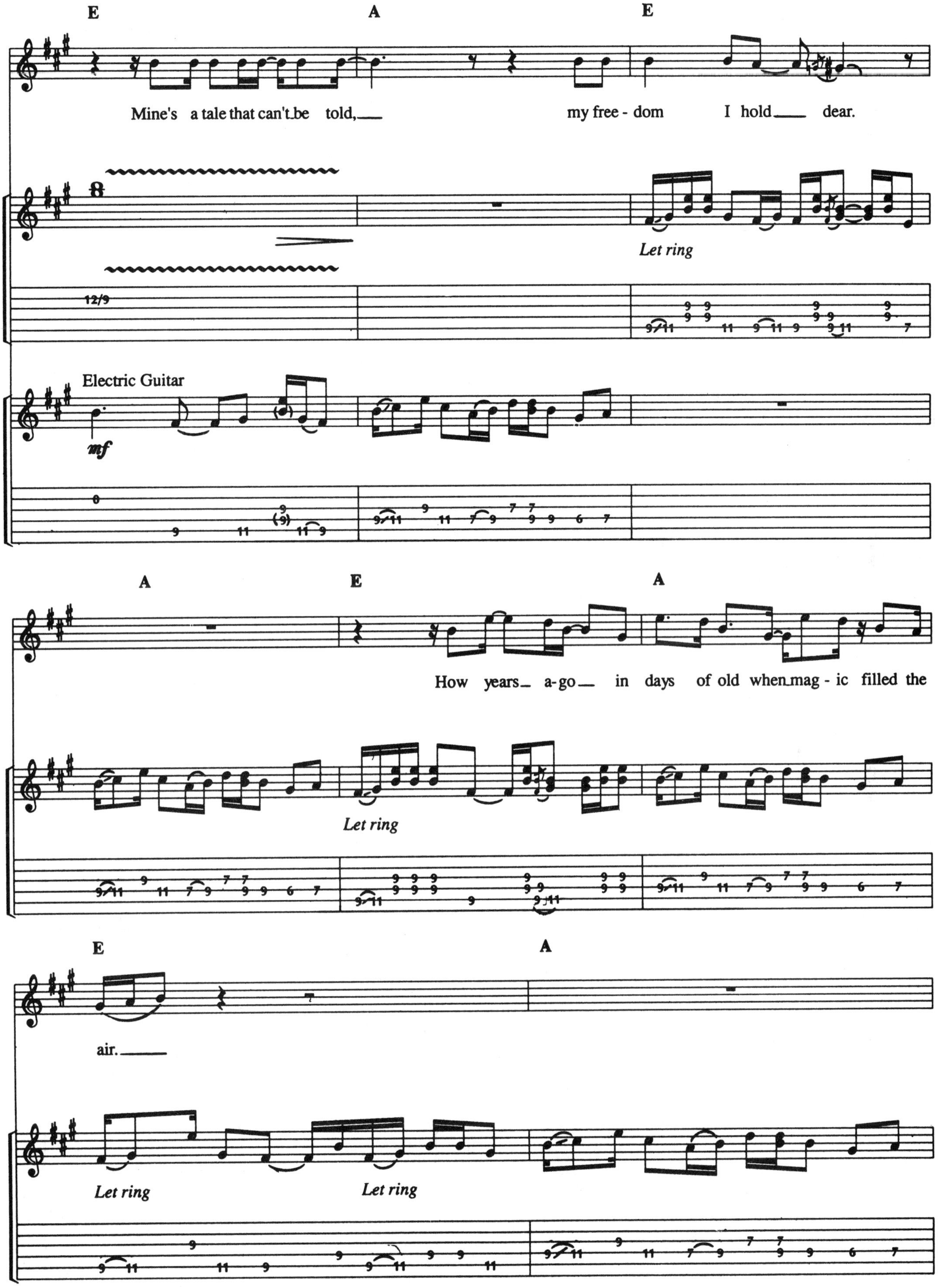

Mine's a tale that can't be told,___ my free-dom I hold___ dear.

Let ring

12/9

Electric Guitar

mf

How years_ a-go_ in days of old when_mag-ic filled the

Let ring

air.___

Let ring   *Let ring*

50

T'was in the dark - est depths of Mor - dor, I met a girl so fair,_____

With Rhythm Figure 1 *(first 7 bars only)*

Let ring   Let ring   Let ring   accel.   Let ring

but Go-lem, the e - vil one,___ crept up and slipped a-

Let ring

way with her_ her_____ her_____ her_____ her,__ Yeah_____

With Rhythm Fill 2

Rhythm Fill 2

Pre-Chorus:

Chorus:
With Rhythm Figure 2 (12times)

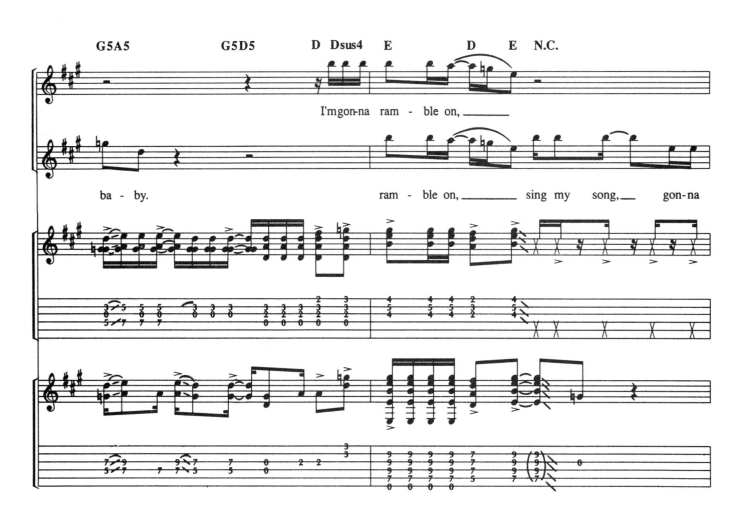

Good Times Bad Times

Words and Music by
JIMMY PAGE, JOHN PAUL JONES,
JOHN BONHAM and ROBERT PLANT

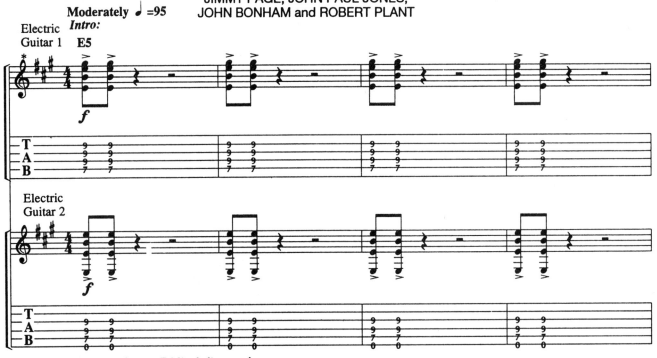

*Key signature indicates E Mixolydian mode.

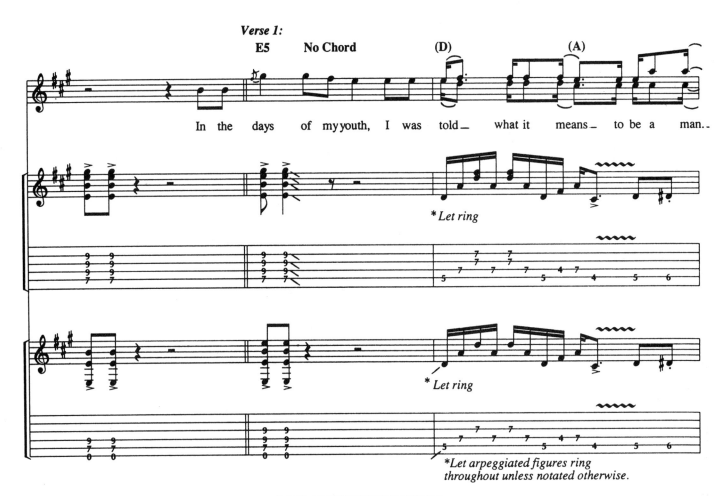

In the days of my youth, I was told __ what it means __ to be a man..

*Let ring

*Let ring

*Let arpeggiated figures ring
throughout unless notated otherwise.

© 1969, 1990 SUPERHYPE PUBLISHING
All rights administered by WB MUSIC CORP.
All Rights Reserved

And now I've reached that age _ I've tried to do _

_____ all those things _ the best I ___ can. _ No
(do ___)

mat-ter how I try__ I find my way in-to the same__ old__ jam.__

Good times, bad__ times,__ you know I've had__ my share.__ Well, my

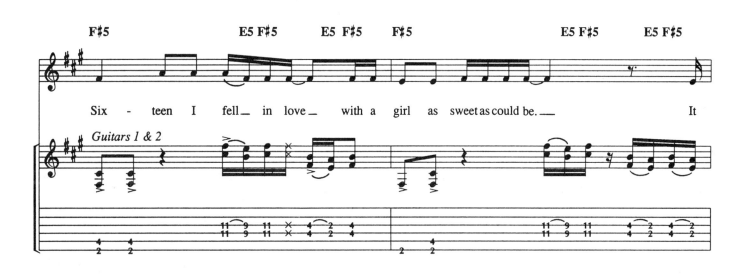

swore that she would be — all mine and love me 'till the end, — but

when I whis-pered in her ear — I lost an-oth-er friend. — Oh!

*Parenthesised notes played by Guitar 1 only

Chorus:

Good times, bad times, — you know I've had my share. — Well, my

Electric Guitar 1

Electric Guitar 2

Let ring   *Let ring*

wo-man left home for a brown-eyed man,____ but I still don't seem to care. ____

Fill 1

Even gliss.

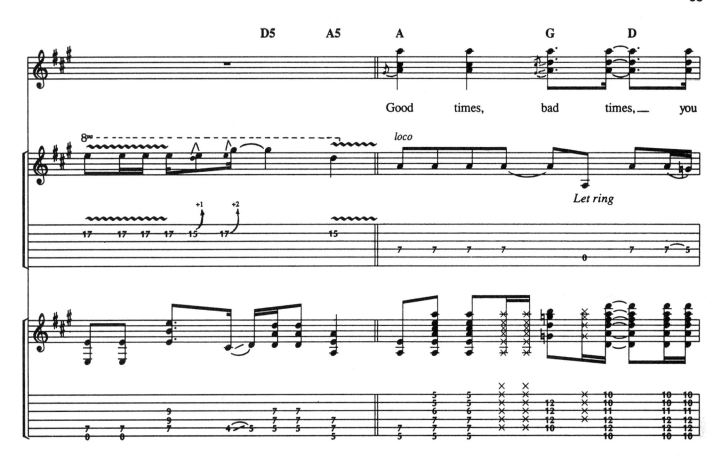

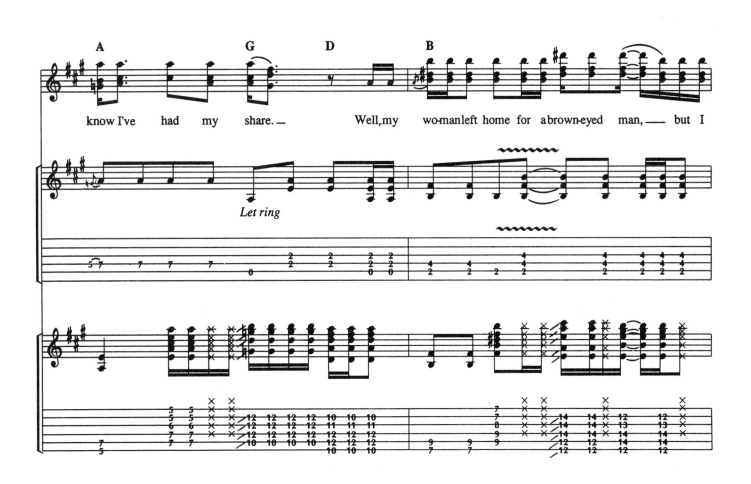

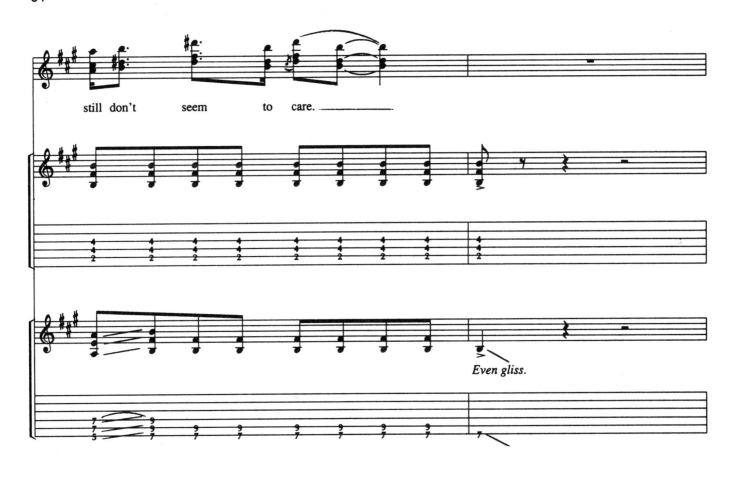

still don't seem to care. _____

Even gliss.

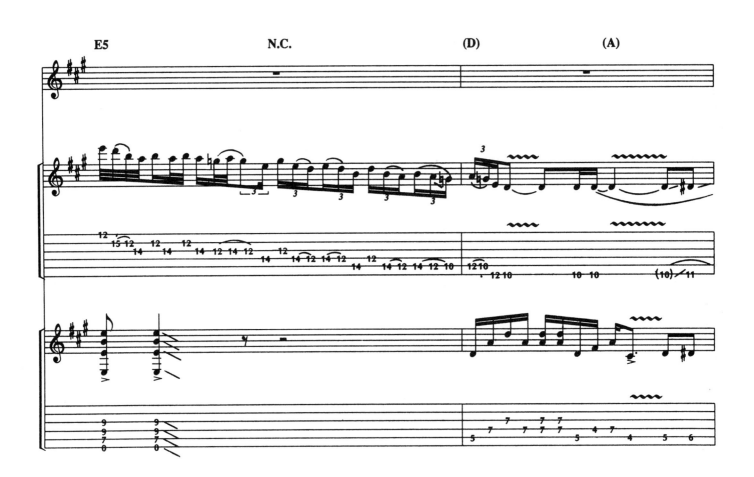

E5   N.C.   (D)   (A)

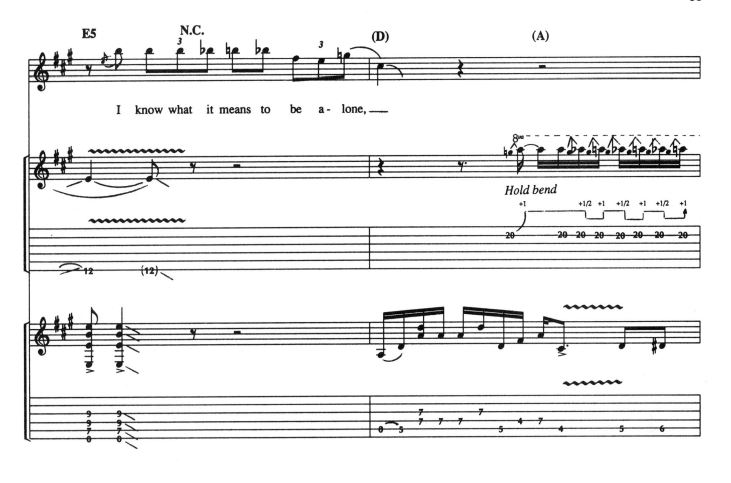

I know what it means to be a - lone, ____

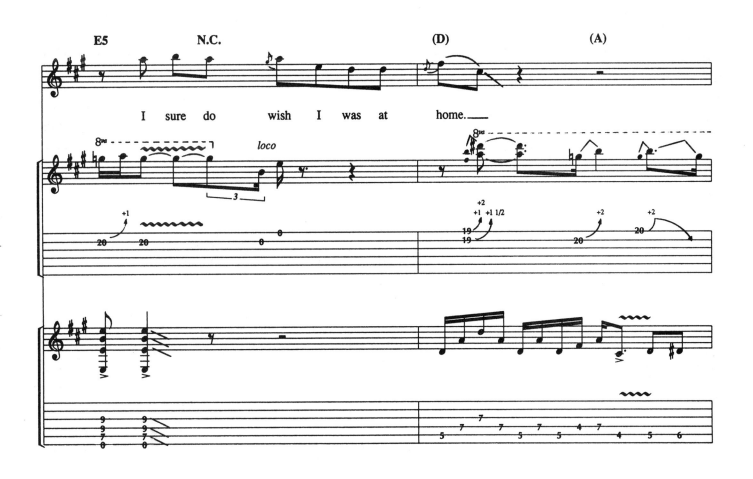

I sure do wish I was at home. ____

66

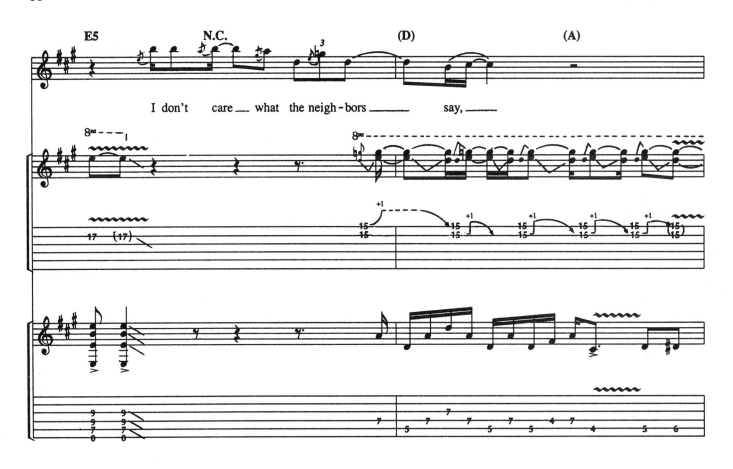

I don't care___ what the neigh-bors ___ say, ___

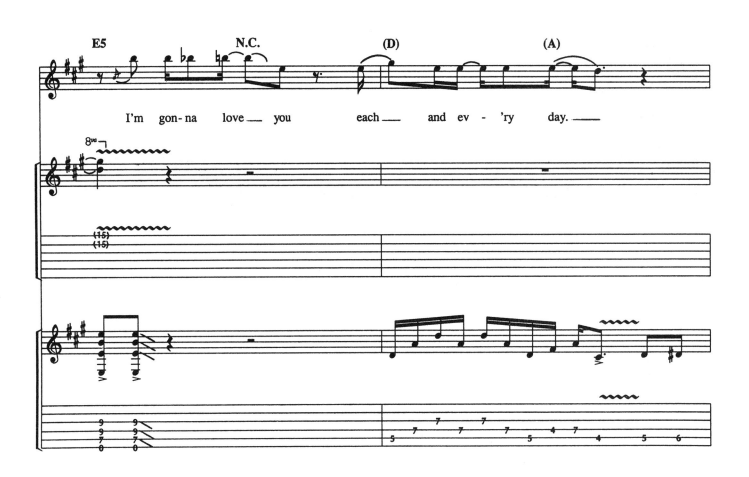

I'm gon-na love___ you each___ and ev - 'ry day. ___

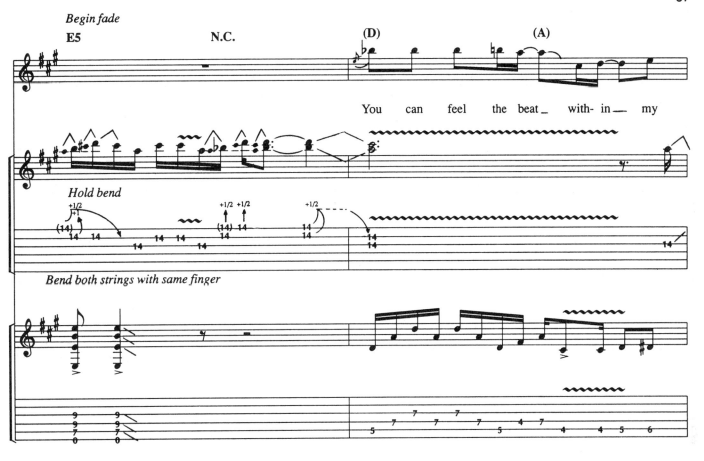

You can feel the beat___ with-in___ my

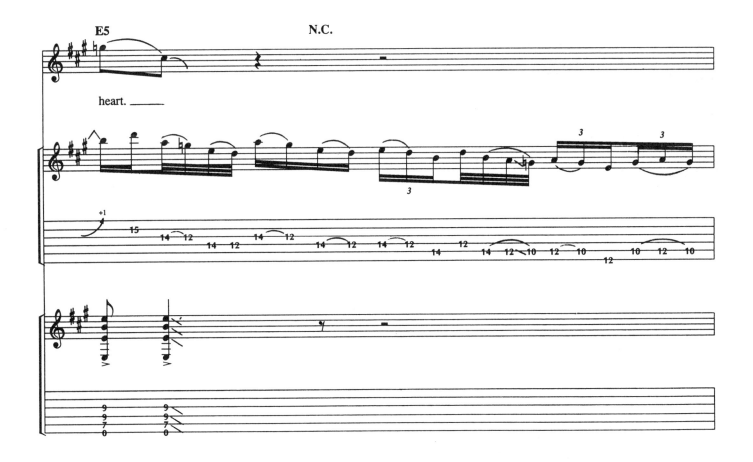

heart. _____

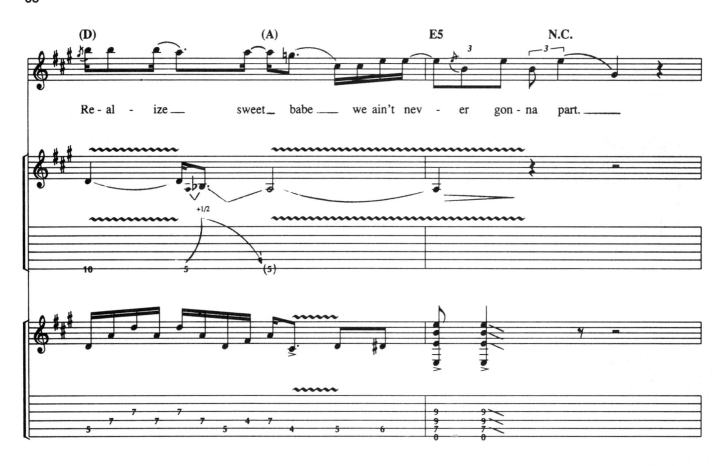

Re - al - ize___ sweet___ babe___ we ain't nev - er gon - na part.___

Fade out

BLACK MOUNTAIN SIDE

Tuning:

⑥ = D ③ = G
⑤ = A ② = A
④ = D ① = D

Music by
JIMMY PAGE

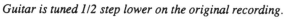

Guitar is tuned 1/2 step lower on the original recording.

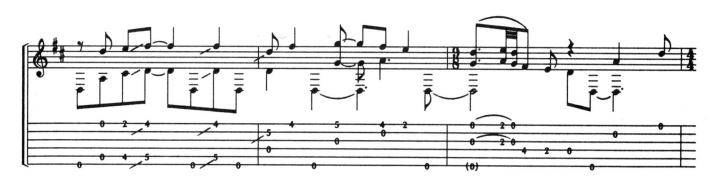

© 1969, 1990 SUPERHYPE PUBLISHING
All rights administered by WB MUSIC CORP.
All Rights Reserved

Let ring

Overdubbed Guitar solo

End solo

Dazed And Confused

Words and Music by
JIMMY PAGE

* Rock wah-wah pedal simile to the following rhythm figure. (+ = treble position, 0 = bass position)

ritard.

© 1969, 1990 SUPERHYPE PUBLISHING
All rights administered by WB MUSIC CORP.
All Rights Reserved

soul of a wo-man was cre-at-ed be-low,_____ yeah._____

*Upstemmed part played through fuzztone with octave effect (8va higher).
This can also be recreated with a pitch transposer.

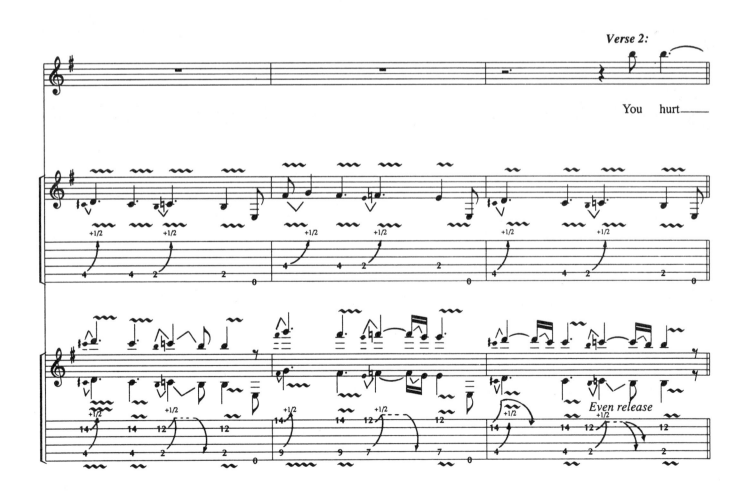

Verse 2:

You hurt_____

_____ and a-bused_____ tell-in' all of your lies.____ Run 'round sweet ba - by, Lord,__ how they hyp-no-tize._

Sweet lit-tle ba - by, I don't know where you been._   Gon - na love you ba - by,   here I come a -

gain.

*Upstemmed part with 8va fuzz

78

Ev - 'ry

Verse 3:

day I work so hard— bring-in' home my hard-earned pay.   Try to love you ba-by, but you push me a- way.——

Don't know where you're go-in', I don't know just where you've been; sweet lit-tle ba-by, I want you a -

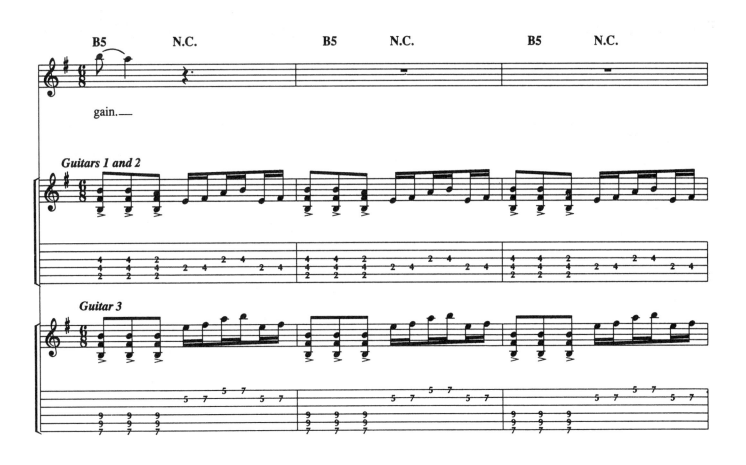

gain.

ah, _____

ah, _____

ah, _____

(ah) ____

Even gliss.

ah, _____

div.

Even gliss.

* Overdubbed fill. Tremelo with bow and wah wah.

ah,   ah,   ah.

Continue tremelo with bow.

yeah!   Al - right!

With wah-wah

Guitar Solo

Ah,   ah,   ah,   ah,   ah,   ah,

ah,   ah,   ah,   ah,   ah.

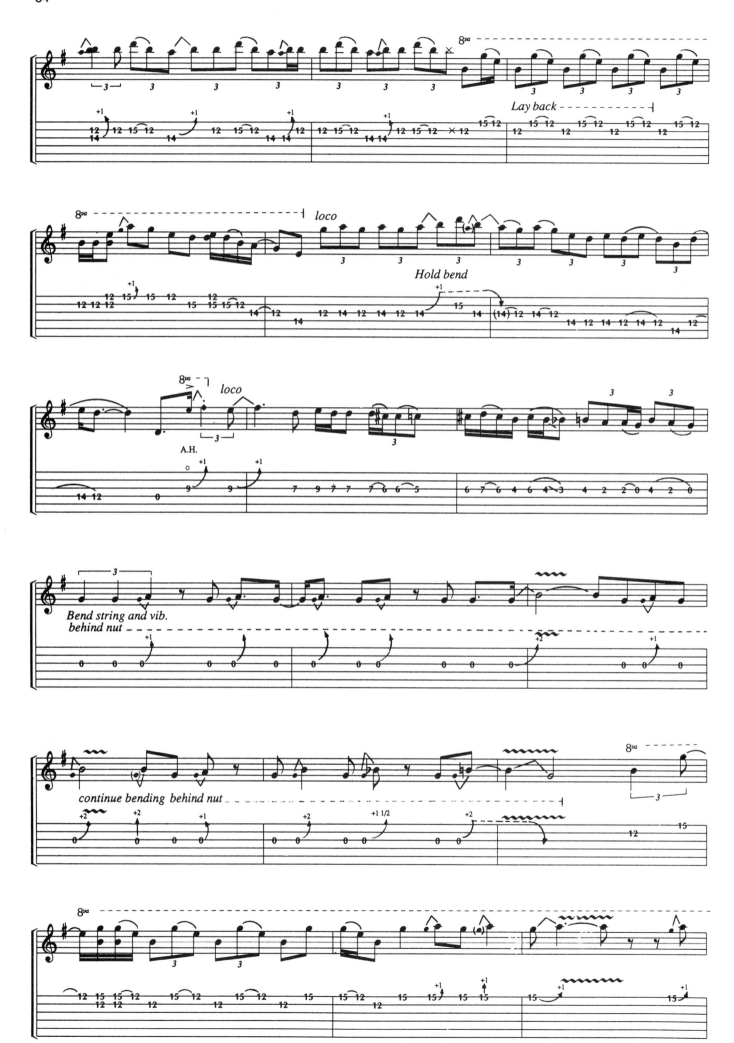

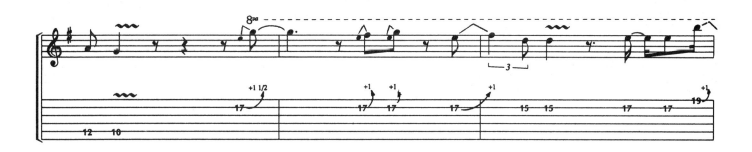

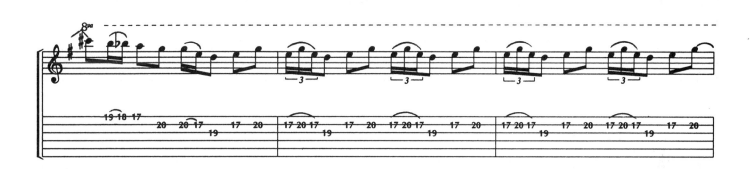

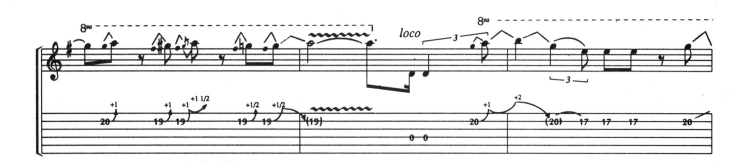

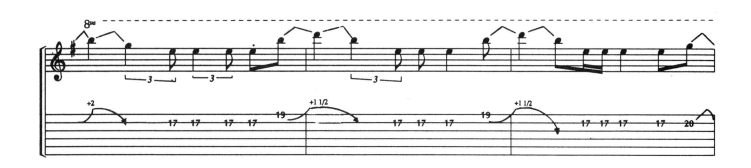

oh ____ don't leave me so con - fused, ____

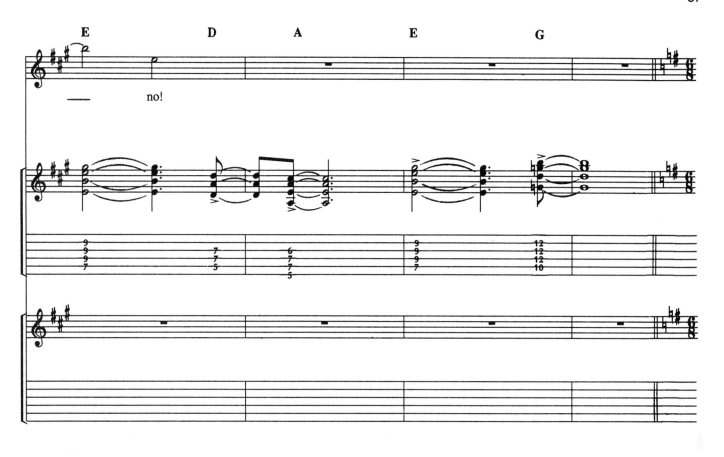

no!

Oh,

ba - by!____

Upstemmed part with 8va fuzz.

Been

dazed and con-fused for so long, it's not true,— want-ed a wo-man nev-er bar-gained for you.—

Take it ea-sy ba-by, let them say what they will.—(Will your) tongue wag so much when I send you the

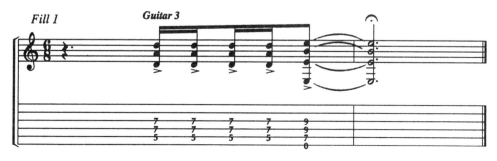

IMMIGRANT SONG

**Words and Music by
JIMMY PAGE and
ROBERT PLANT**

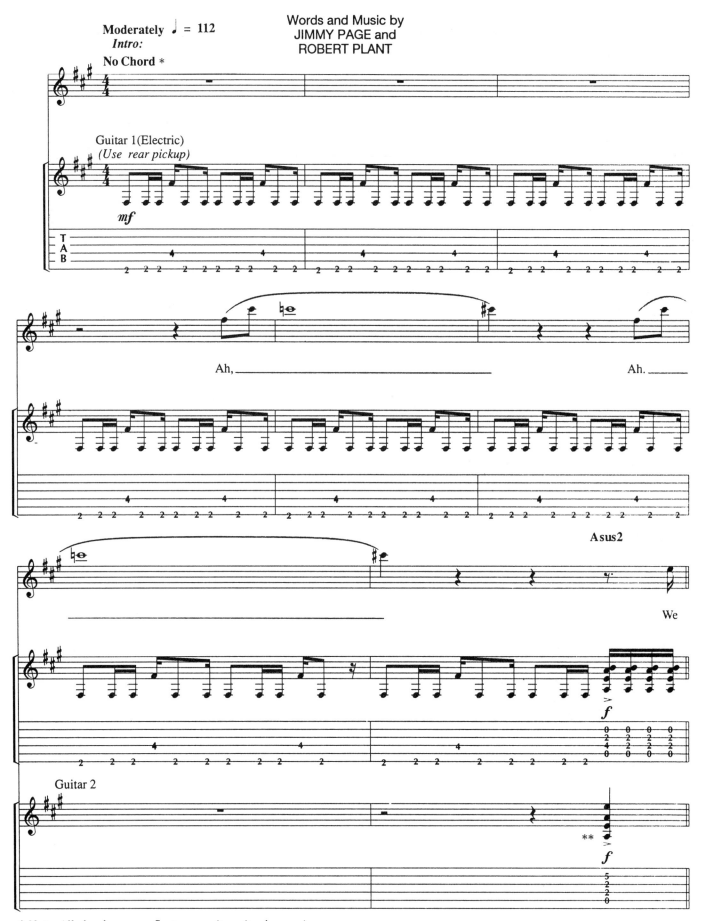

* *Note: All chord names reflect composite guitar harmonies.*
** *With amplifier vibrato set to 16th note pulse.*

© 1970, 1991 SUPERHYPE PUBLISHING
All rights administered by WB MUSIC CORP.
All Rights Reserved

Verse 1:

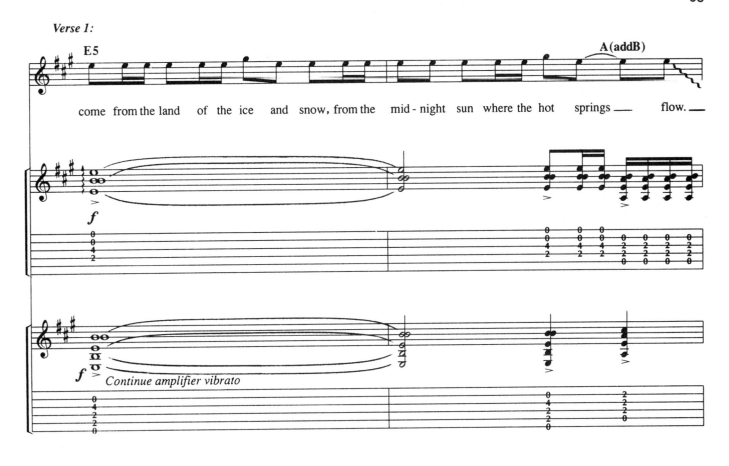

come from the land of the ice and snow, from the mid-night sun where the hot springs ___ flow. ___

Continue amplifier vibrato

___ Ham-mer of ___ the gods, will drive our ships to new ___

Guitar 1

Guitar 3 *(Guitar 2 tacet)*

*** Muted scratch/strum—roughly parallels the bass part.*

F♯(addG♯)

land.____ To fight the hordes ___ and

A5   E5   A

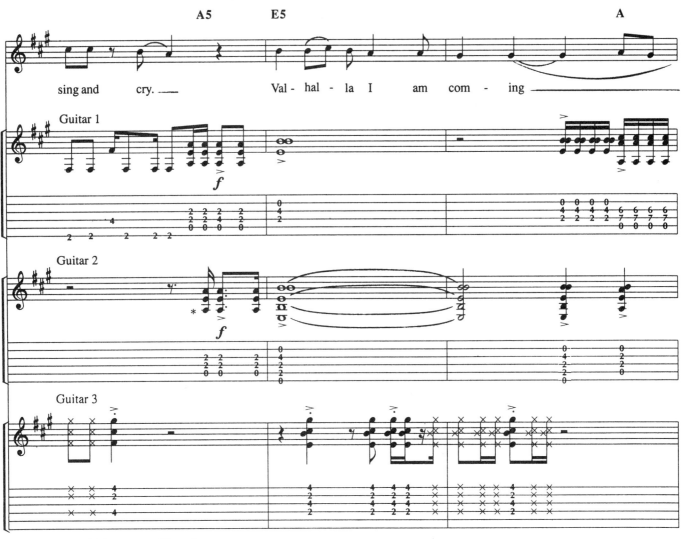

sing and   cry. ____   Val - hal - la I   am com - ing _____

Guitar 1

Guitar 2

Guitar 3

Return 16th note amplifier vibrato

Al - ways sweep   with,   with thresh- ing oar. _____

Guitar 1 *(Tripletracked)*

Guitar 3 *(Guitar 2 tacet)*

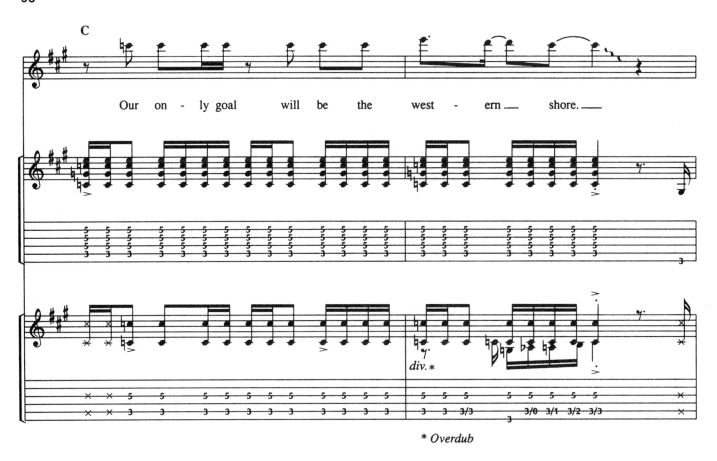

C

Our on - ly goal will be the west - ern shore.

Overdub

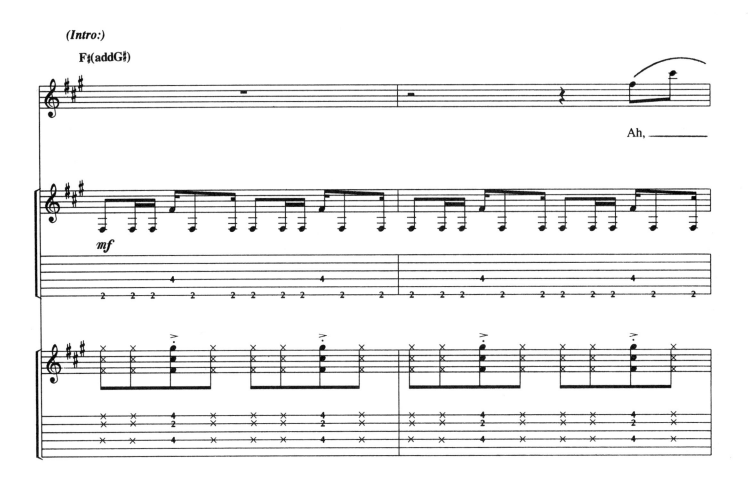

(Intro:)

F#(addG#)

Ah,

mf

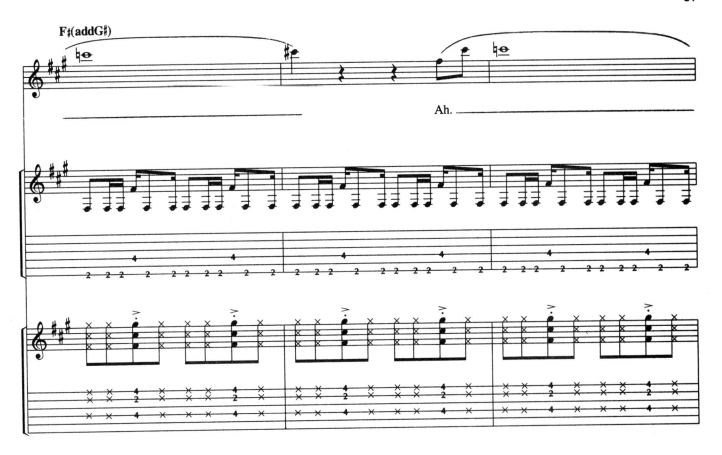

Verse 2:

A5   E5

We come from the land of the ice and snow, from the

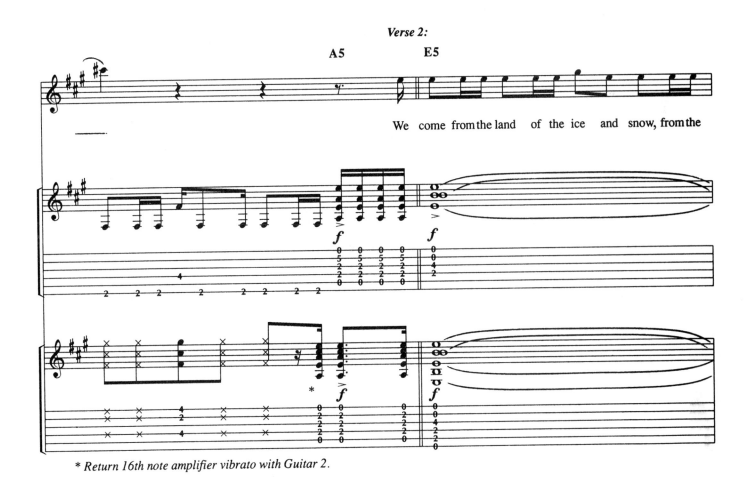

* Return 16th note amplifier vibrato with Guitar 2.

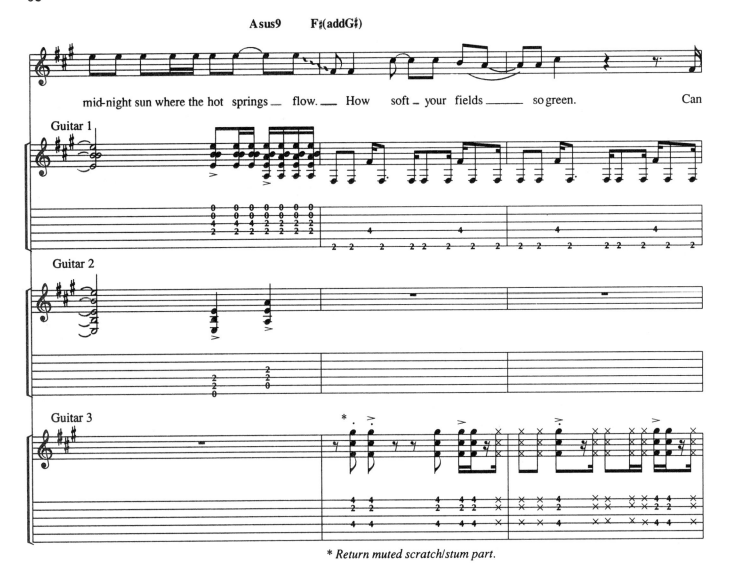

Asus9   F#(addG#)

mid-night sun where the hot springs __ flow. __ How soft _ your fields _____ so green.   Can

Guitar 1

Guitar 2

Guitar 3

* Return muted scratch/stum part.

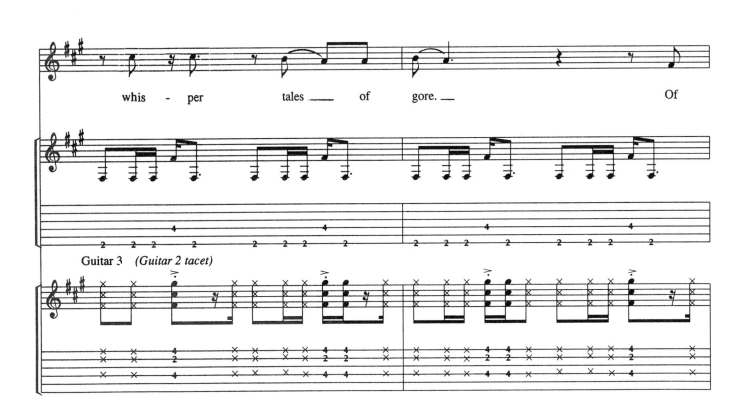

whis - per   tales ___ of   gore. ___   Of

Guitar 3   (Guitar 2 tacet)

how we calmed ___ the tides of war. ___ We are ___ your

* Return 16th note amplifier vibrato.

ov - er Lords. ___

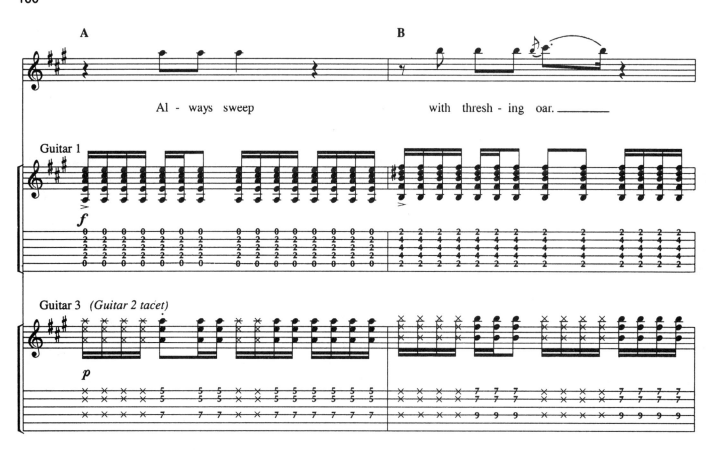

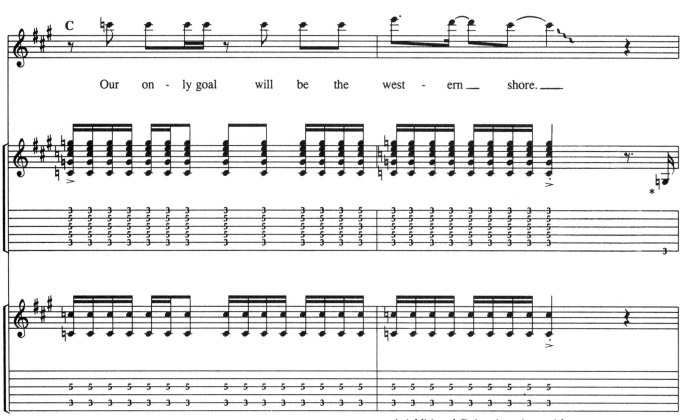

*Additional Guitar in unison with
original (treble pick-up with distortion.)*

F♯(addG♯)

So

now you'd bet-ter stop, ___ and re-build all ___ your ru-ins. For

* Upstemmed part on beats 3&4: additional guitar fill.

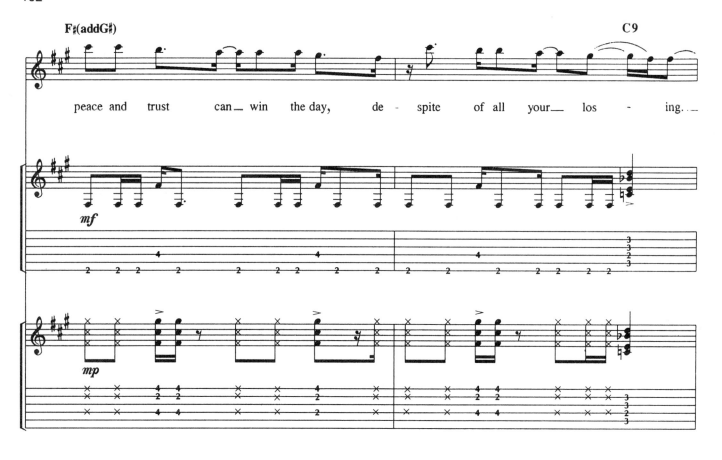

peace and trust can win the day, de - spite of all your los - ing.

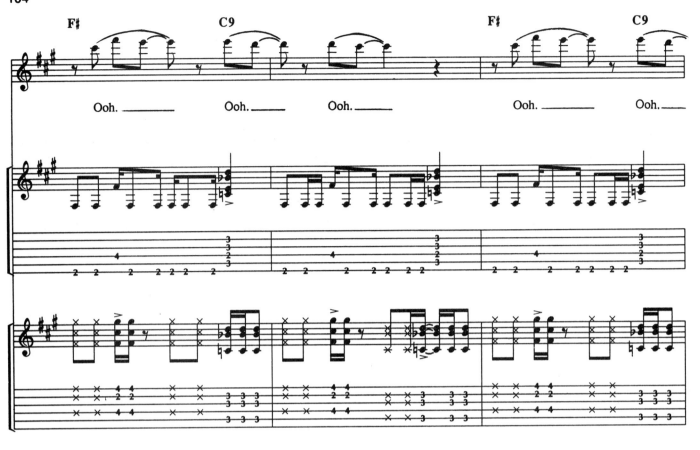

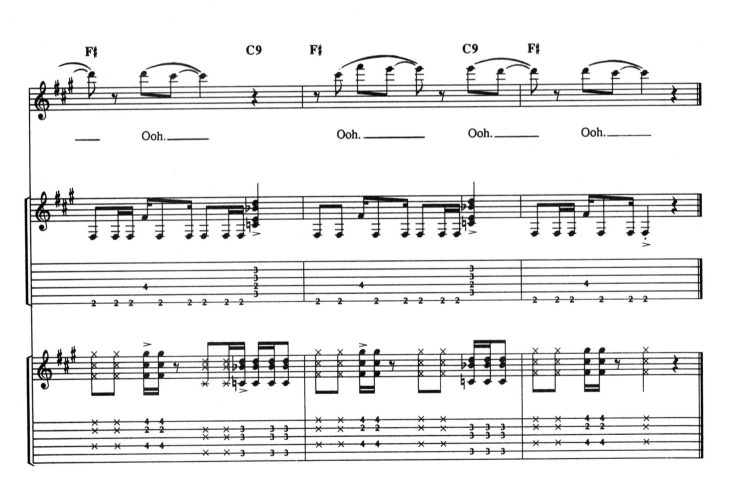

Stairway To Heaven

Words and Music by
JIMMY PAGE and
ROBERT PLANT

*Capo at VII using a cutaway guitar with easy access to the 22nd fret. All notes in TAB at VII are open strings.

**The open first string is not played here, but rings sympathetically.

***A gradual decrescendo continues for the next four measures to allow for the entrance of the recorders.

© 1972, 1992 SUPERHYPE PUBLISHING
All rights administered by WB MUSIC CORP.
All Rights Reserved

*The actual pitch of this note(e) is one octave higher

buy - ing___ the stair-way to heav - (en.) When she gets there she knows___ if the

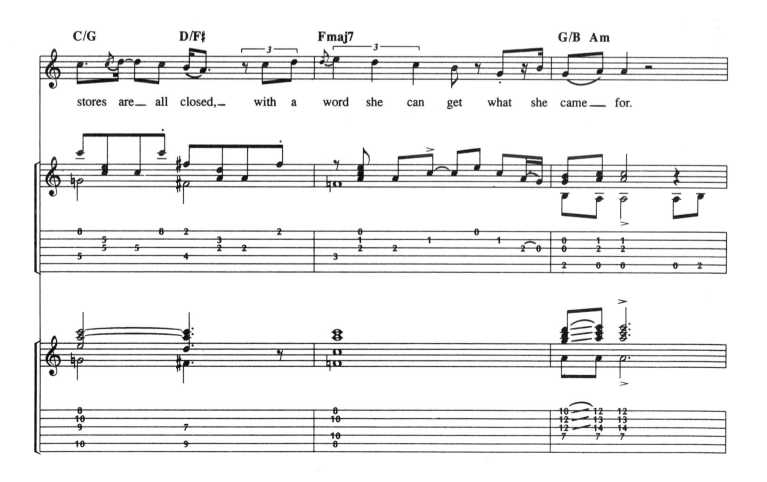

stores are___ all closed,___ with a word she can get what she came___ for.

108

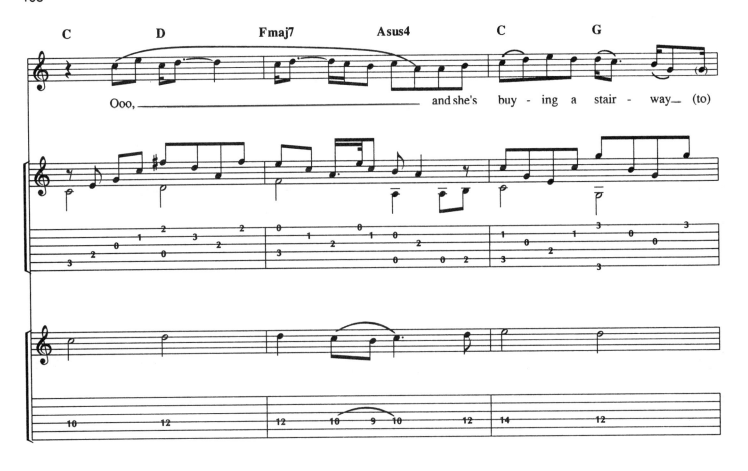

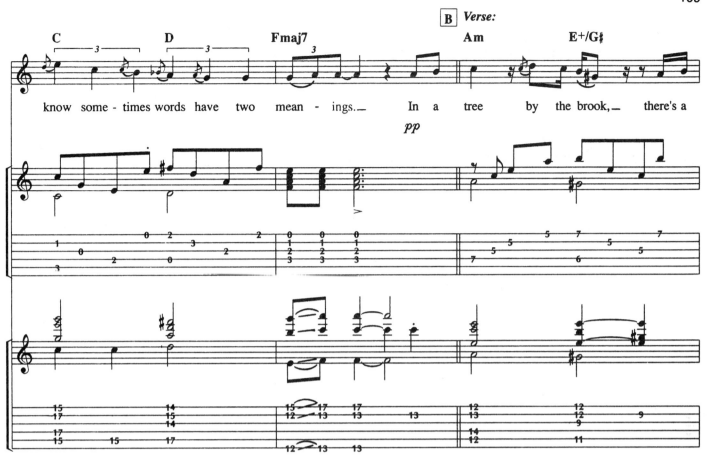

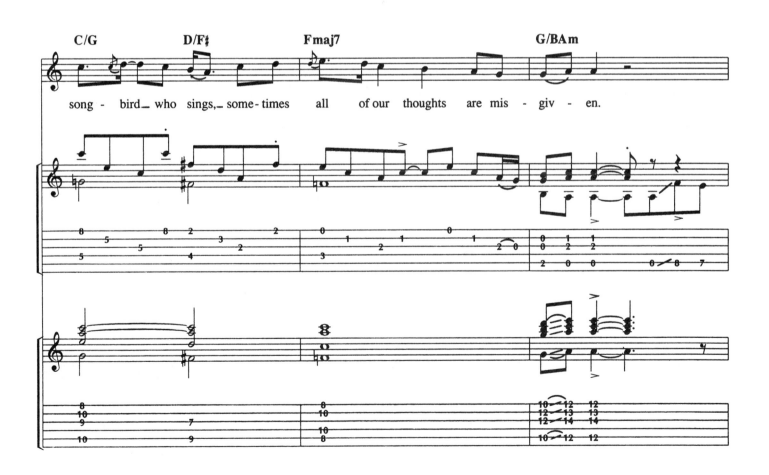

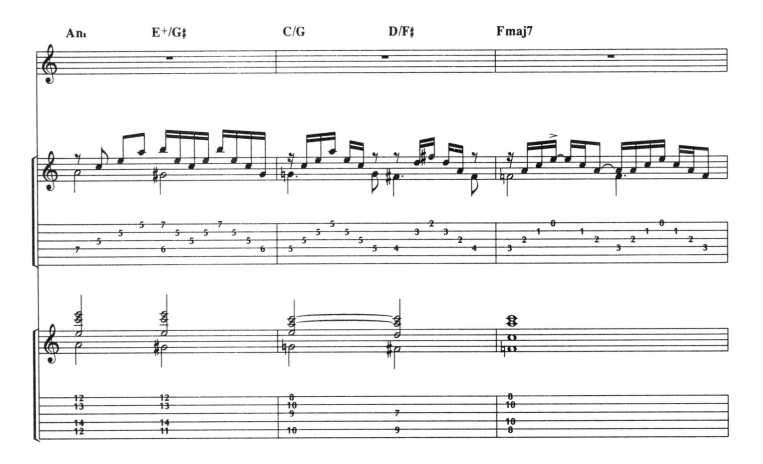

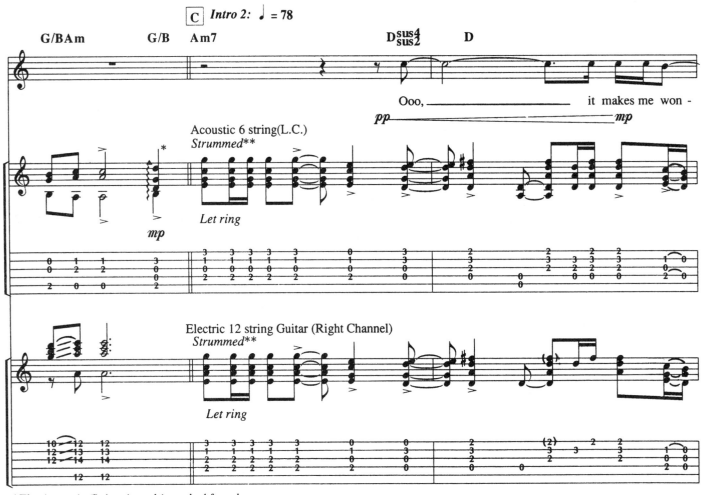

*The Acoustic Guitar is multi-tracked from here on.
**With a pick.

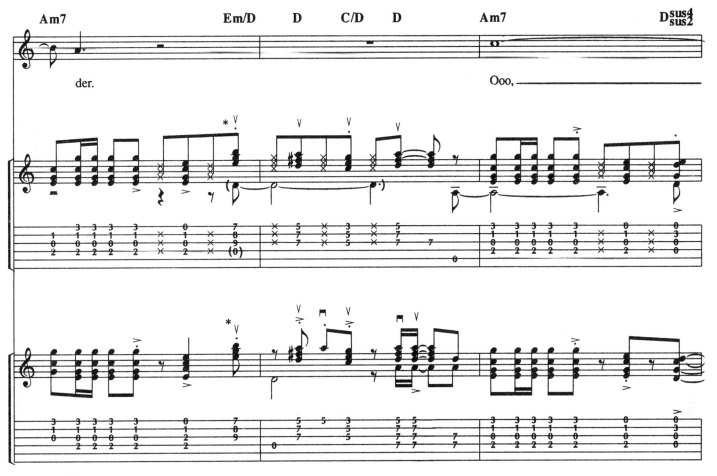

*Suggested strum

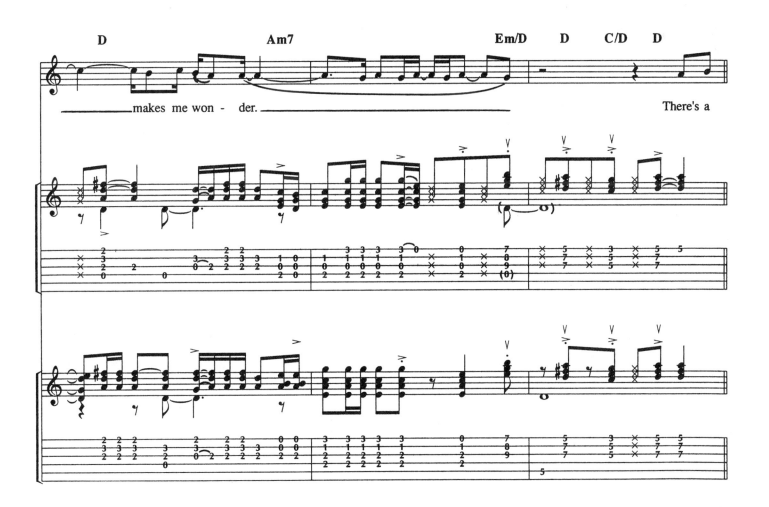

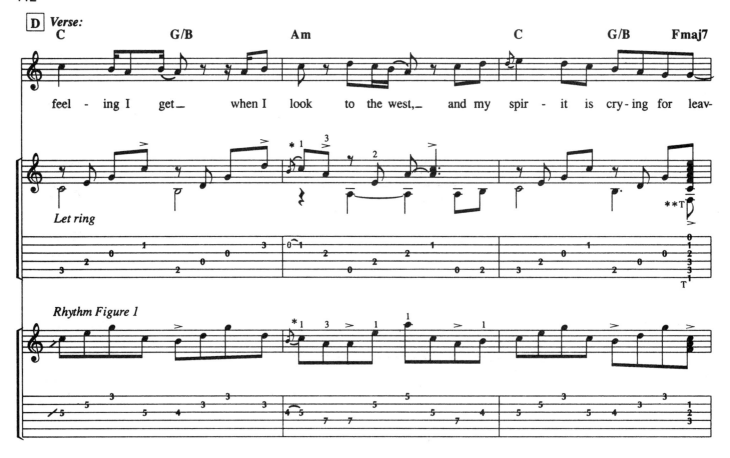

feel - ing I get___ when I look to the west,___ and my spir - it is cry-ing for leav-

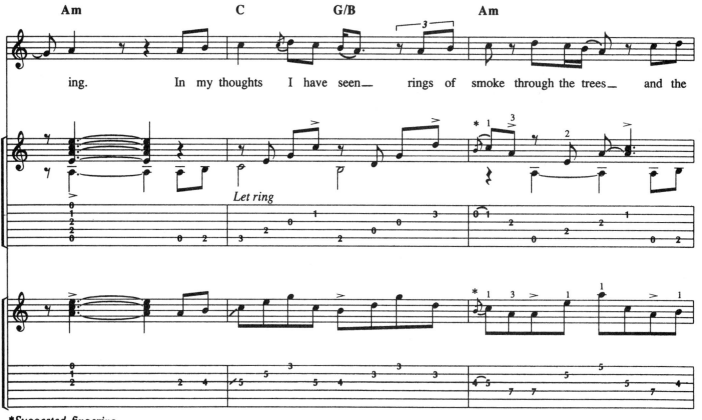

ing. In my thoughts I have seen___ rings of smoke through the trees___ and the

*Suggested fingering.

**T=Thumb on ⑥

Strings ④ and ② are muted while ③ and ① are open.

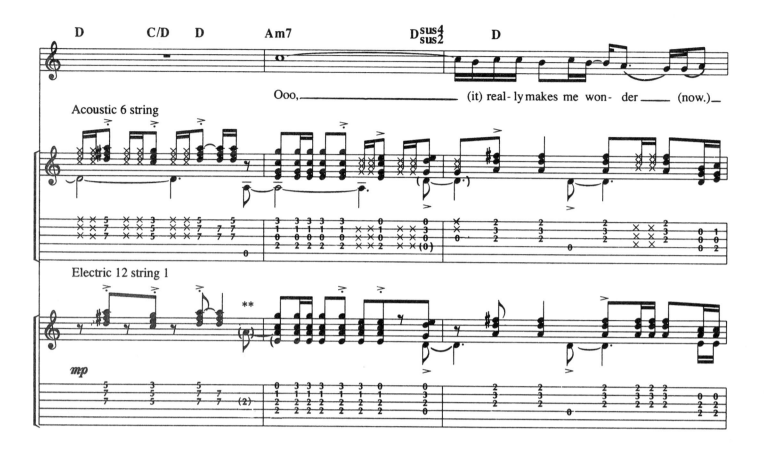

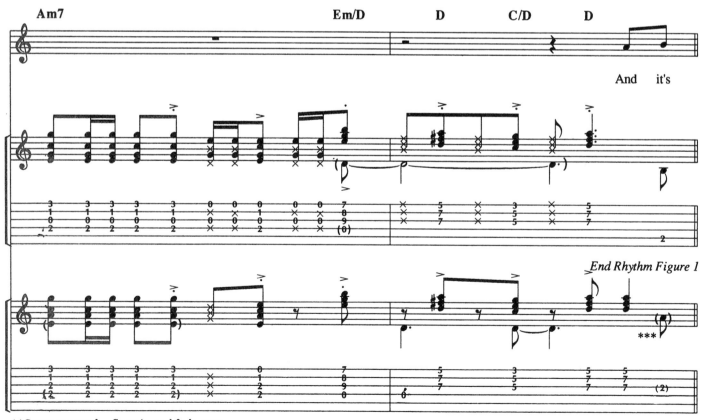

Separate track – Sustain and fade over.

Separate track.

116

*Doubled with an Electric 6 string (Telecaster?) from here on.

**( ) Acoustic Guitar track only.

118

the pip - er's call-ing you__ to join__ him.

Dear la - dy can you hear the wind-

blow, and did you__ know,__ your stair- way lies on the whis - 'prin' wind. _____

Rhythm figure 1 out

Oh. _____

Acoustic Guitar (L.C.)

cresc.

Electric 12 string (R&LC)

cresc.

**The tempo is resumed by a cue from the guitarist.

*Notes in parenthesis are upper notes of quieter background track.

I *Bridge:(Guitar Solo)*

*Electric 6 string Guitar 1 (R & LC)

*1958 Telecaster through a Fender Suproamp?

** *punch in from a separate track*

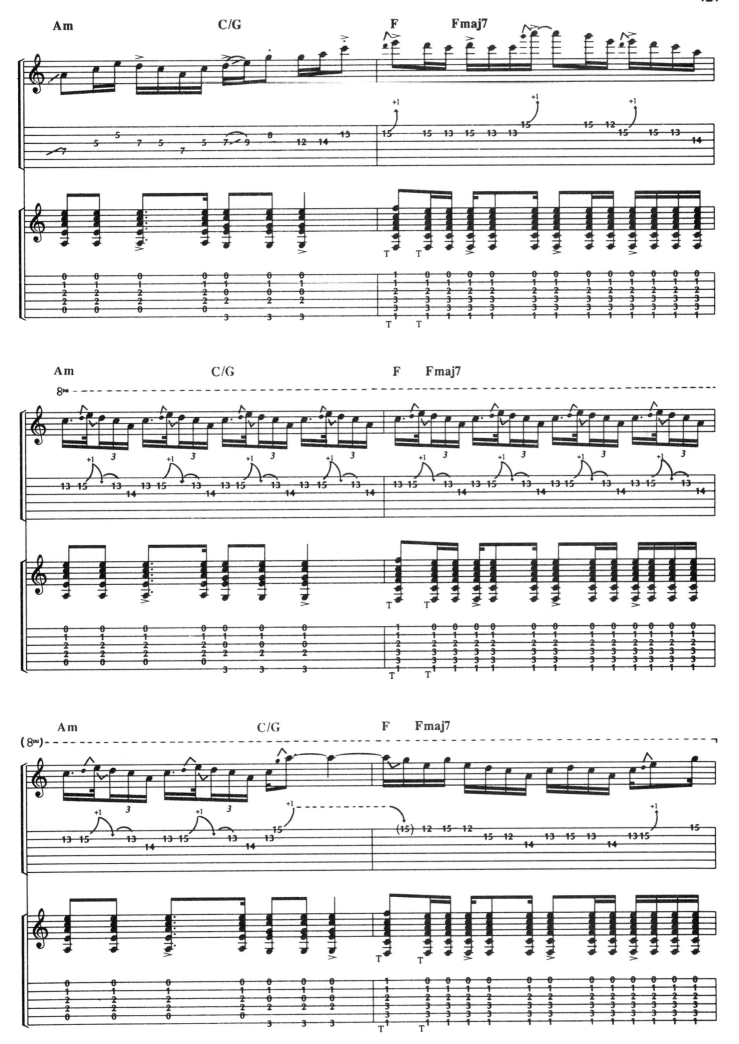

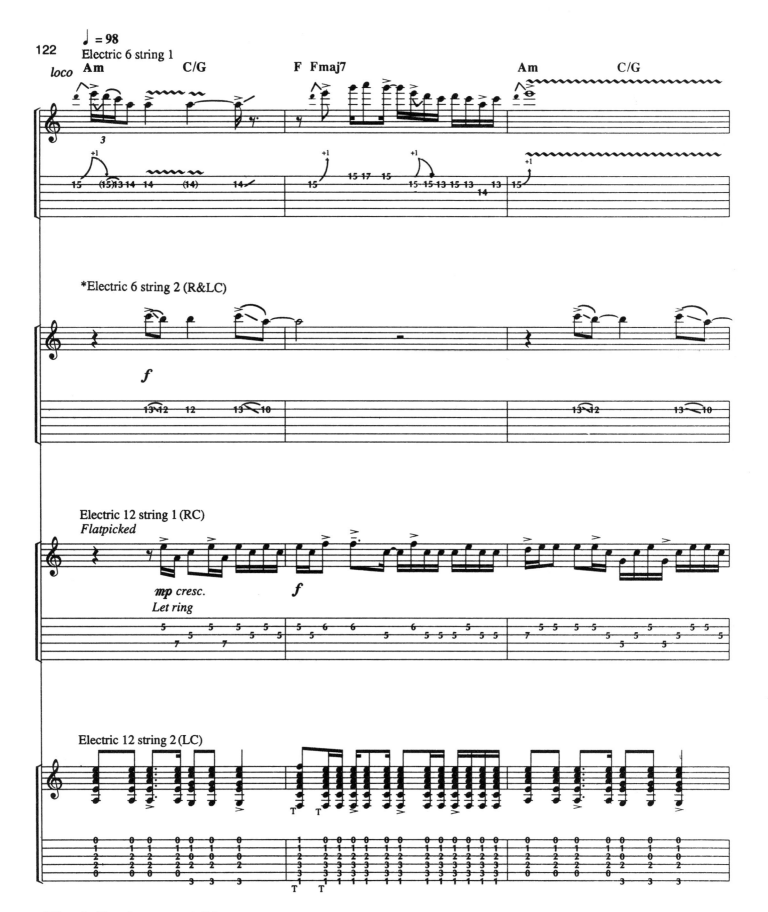

*Played with a glass or metal slide.

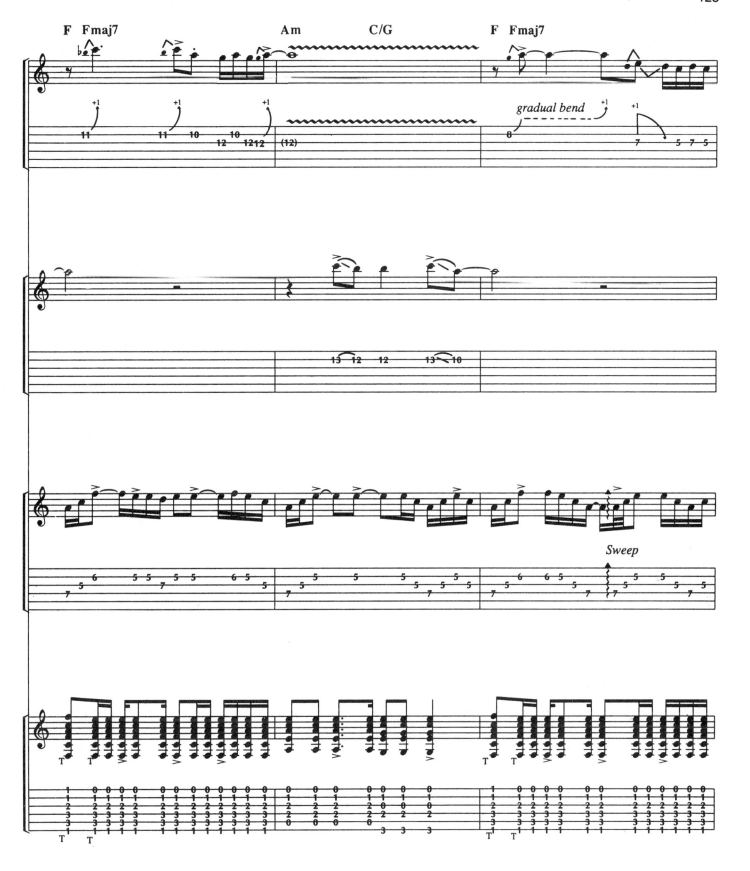

J *Verse:* *With Rhythm Figure 3 with ad lib variations*

♩ = 102

Am   G5   F   G(addA) Am   G5

Vocals 8ᵛᵃ (doubled)

And as we wind on down the road,   our shad-ows tal-ler than our soul,

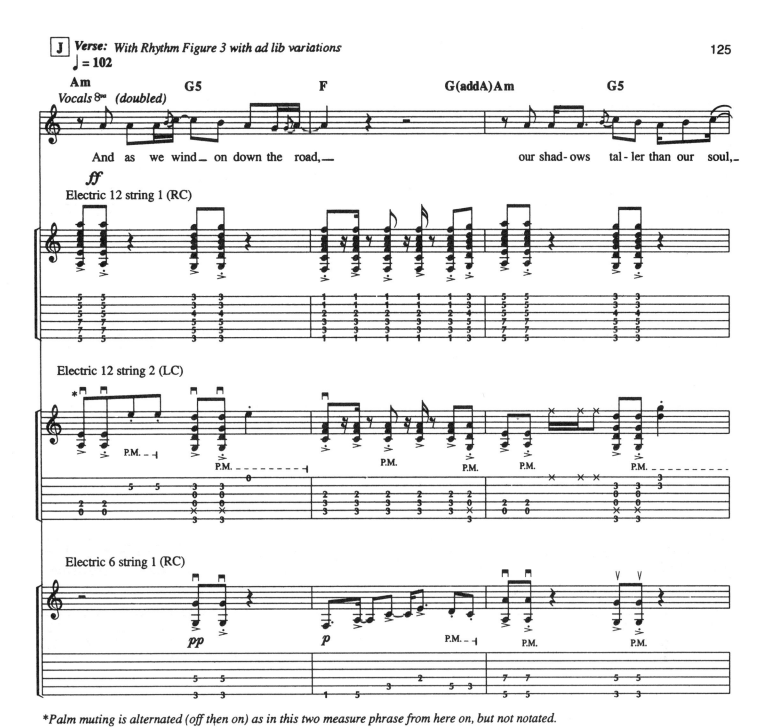

Electric 12 string 1 (RC)

Electric 12 string 2 (LC)

Electric 6 string 1 (RC)

*Palm muting is alternated (off then on) as in this two measure phrase from here on, but not notated.

Rhythm Figure 3
Electric 12 string Guitar 3 (RC)

*Mute strings with fret hand at current chord position.

126

Right and left channels from here on.

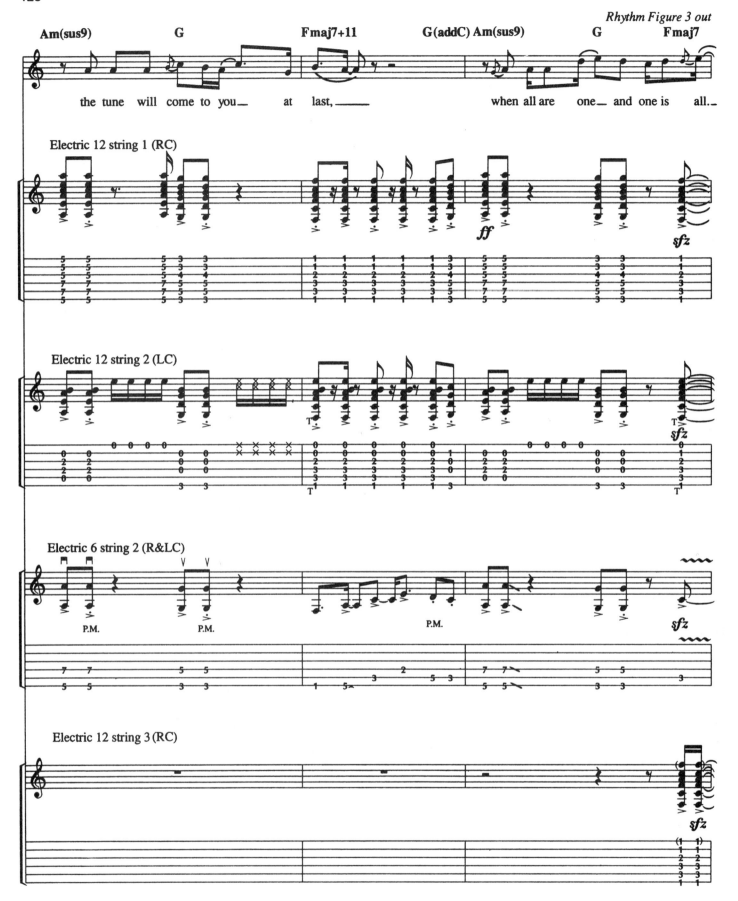

the tune will come to you at last, when all are one and one is all.

*Pan to center.
**Doubling ends.

130

Lead vocal in downstems, distorted chorus track in upstems.

*Pre-bent from here on

132

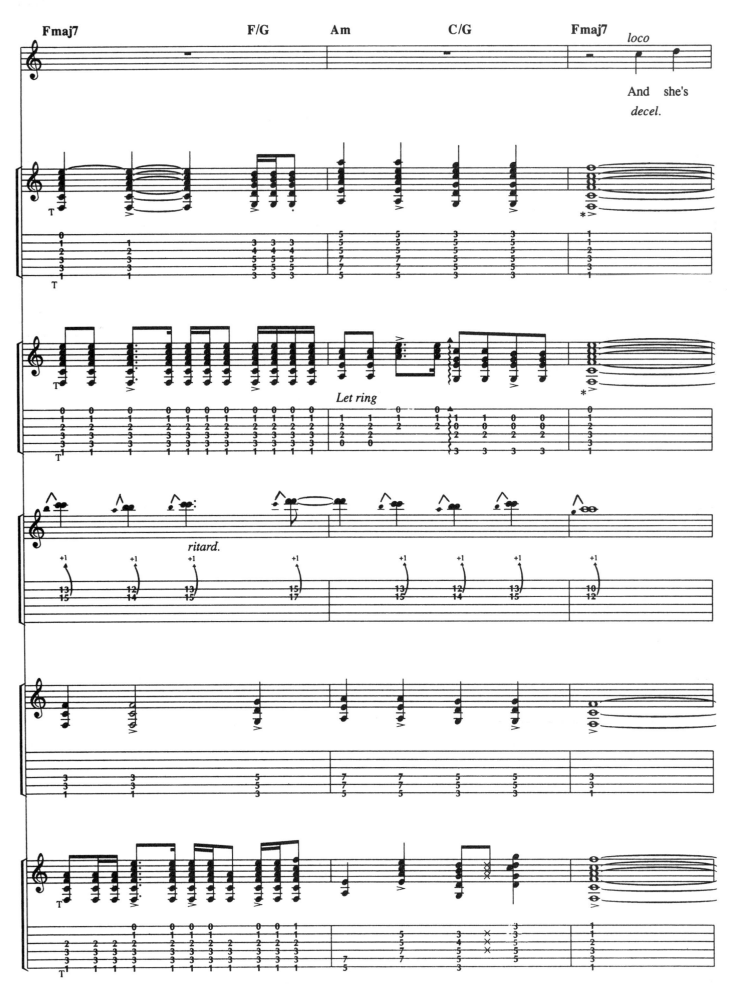

*VSO (variable speed/pitch oscilator) 1/2 step glide.

Oscillate guitar volume knob rhythmically.

Communication Breakdown

Fast Rock ♩ = 174

Words and Music by
JIMMY PAGE , ROBERT PLANT,
JOHN BONHAM and JOHN PAUL JONES

© 1969, 1990 SUPERHYPE PUBLISHING
All rights administered by WB MUSIC CORP.
All Rights Reserved

Verse 1:

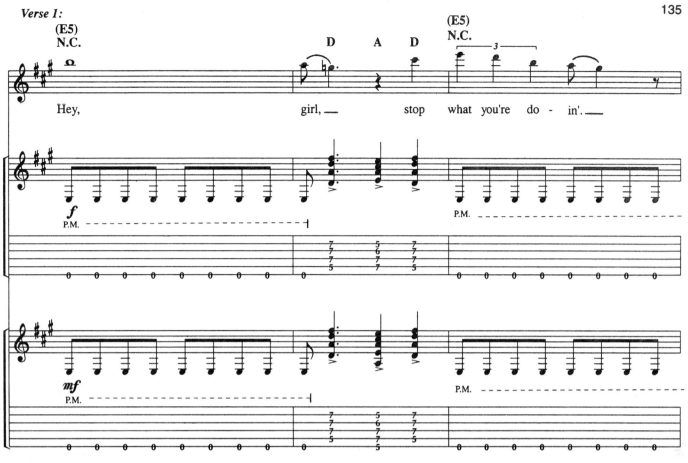

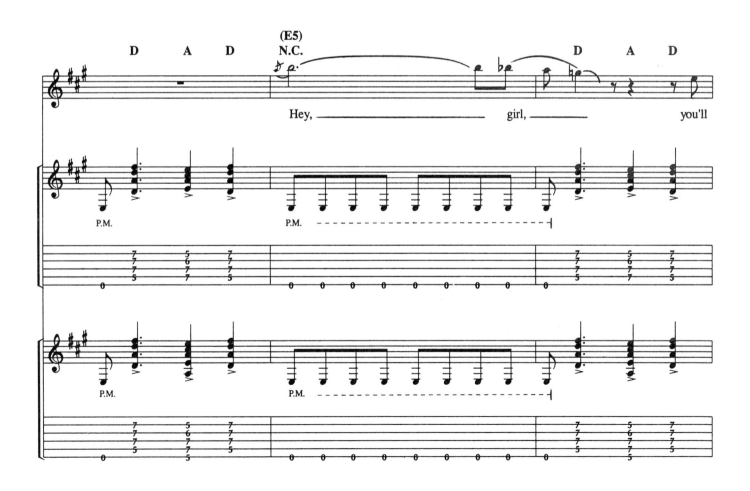

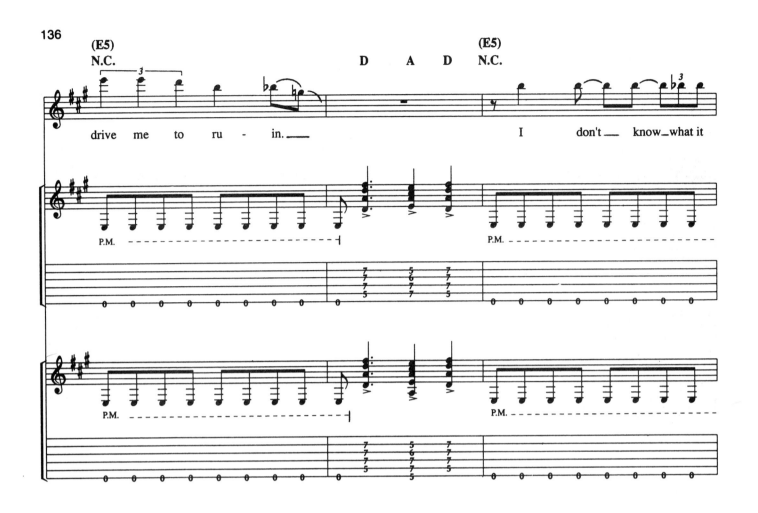

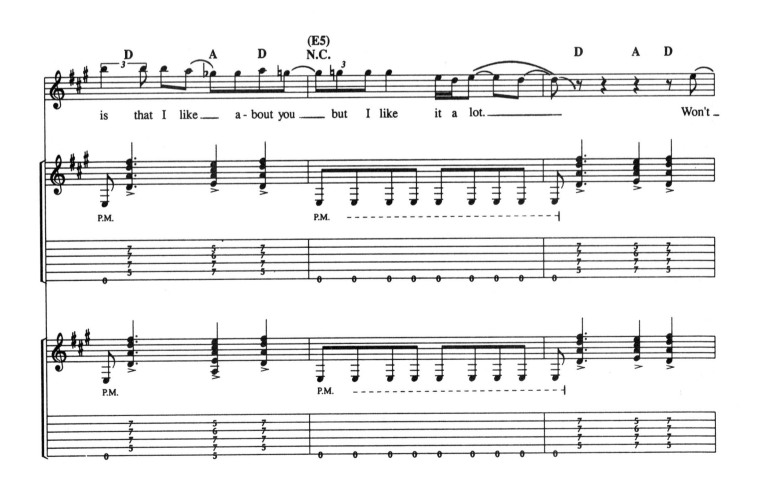

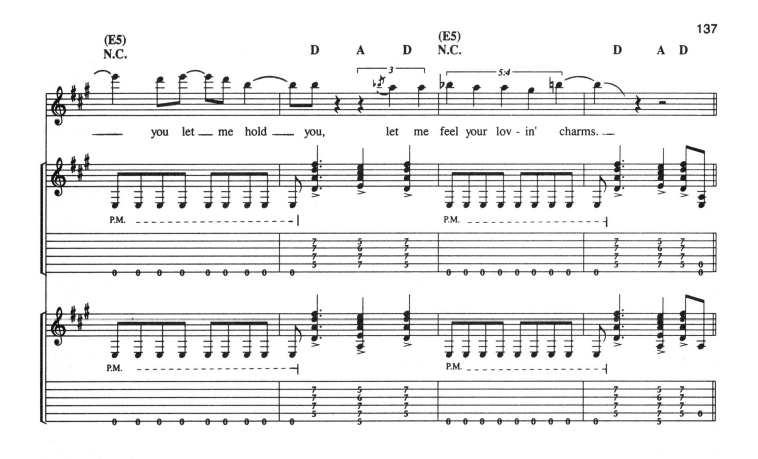

Chorus:

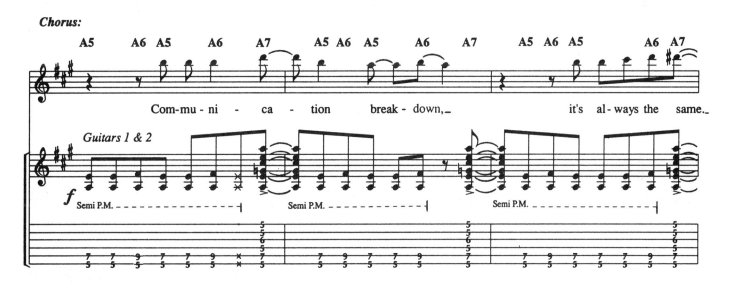

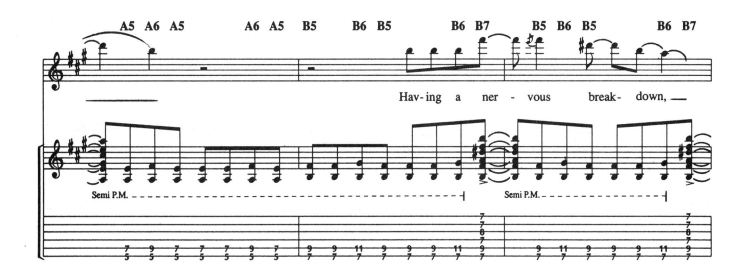

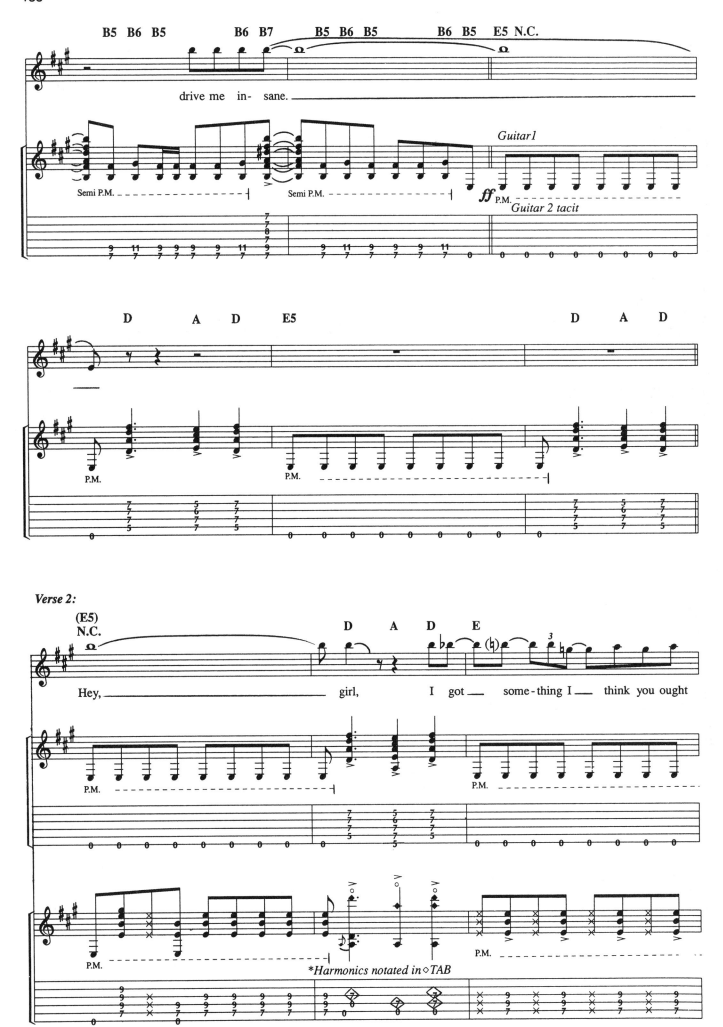

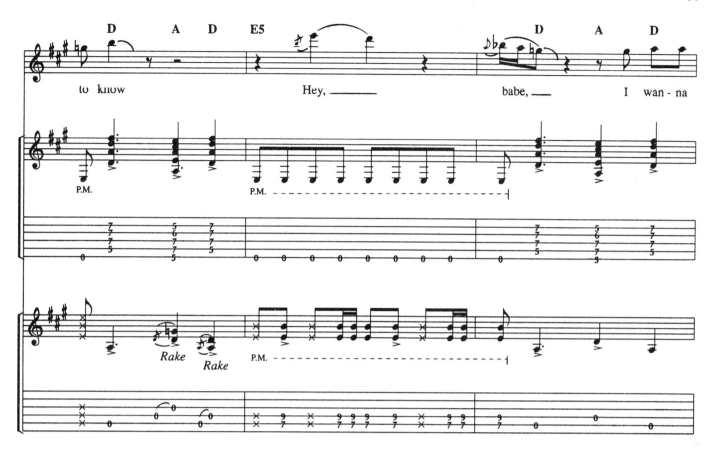

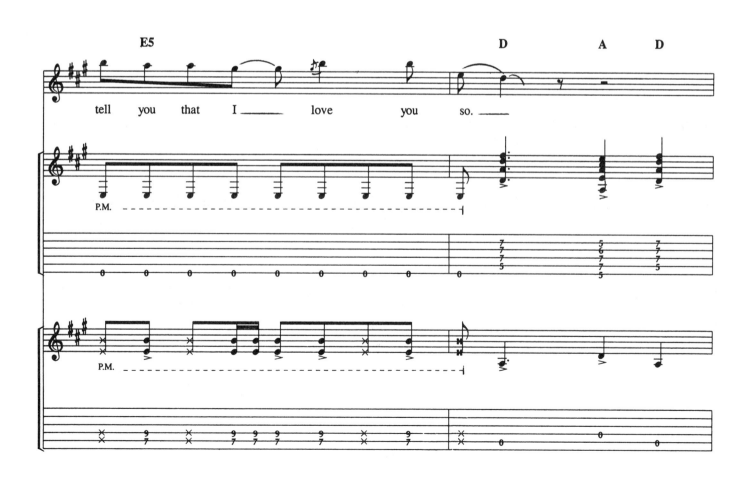

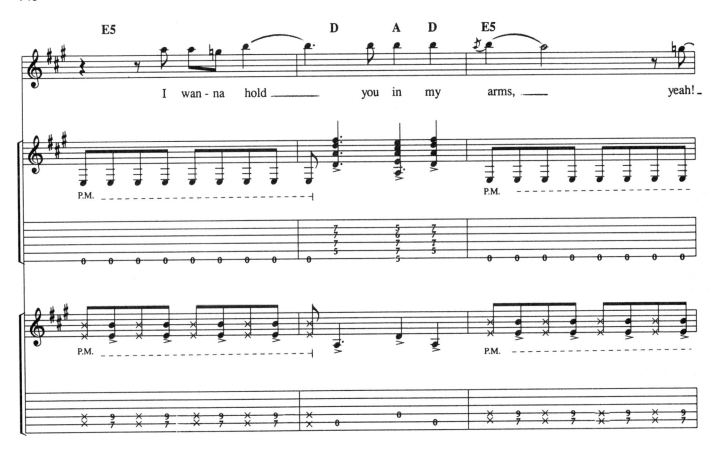

I wan-na hold _____ you in my arms, _____ yeah!

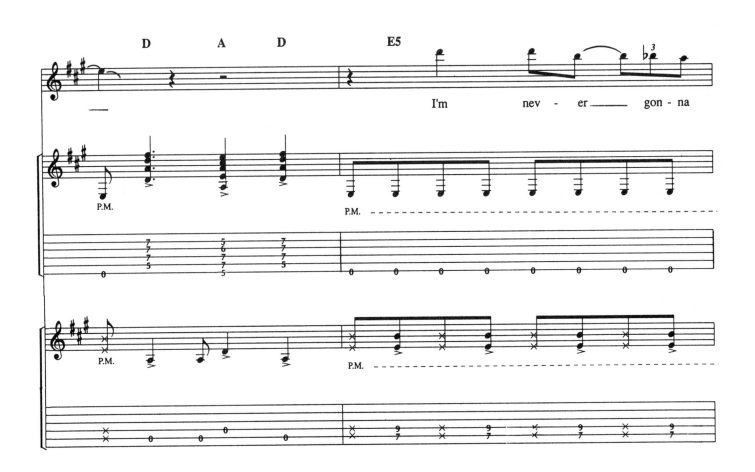

I'm nev - er _____ gon - na

Chorus:

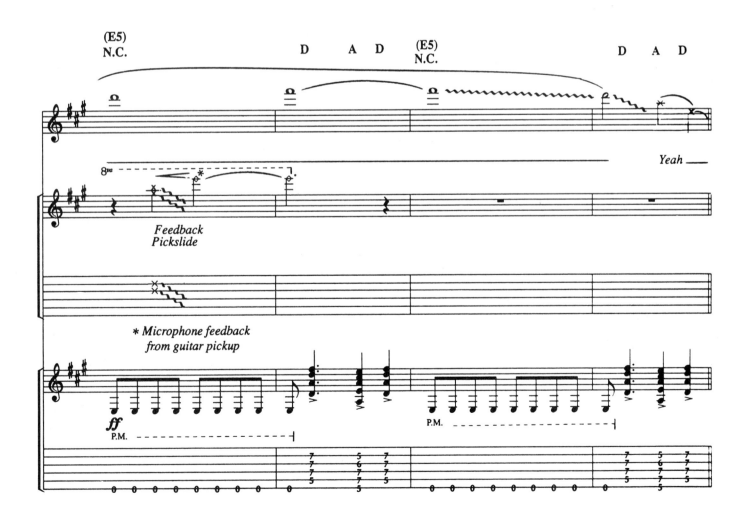

Refrain:

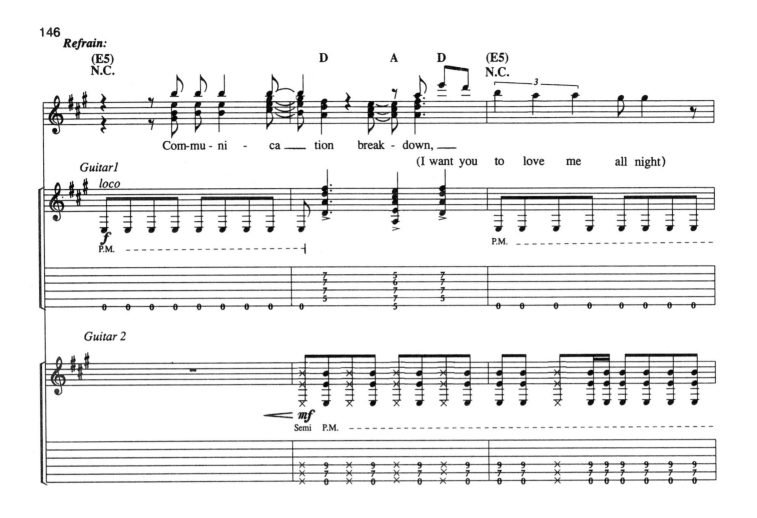

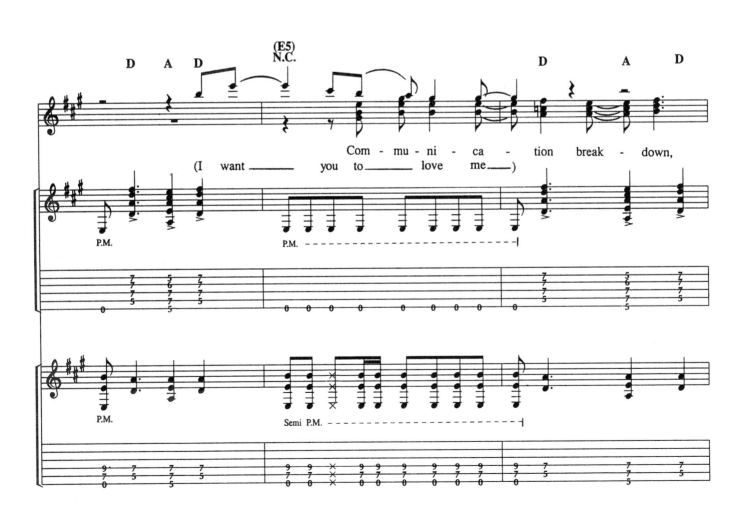

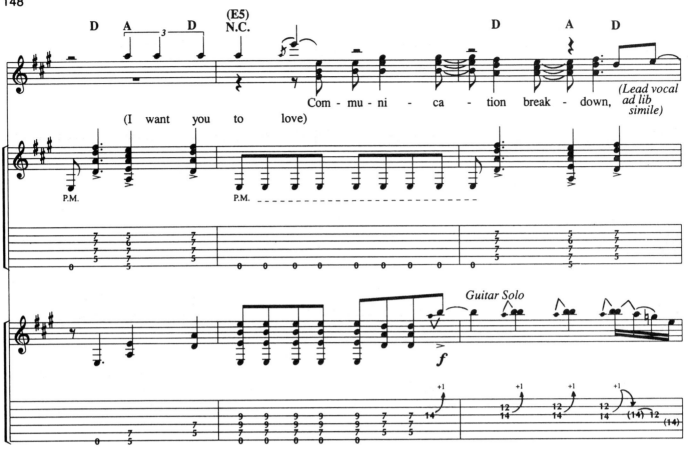

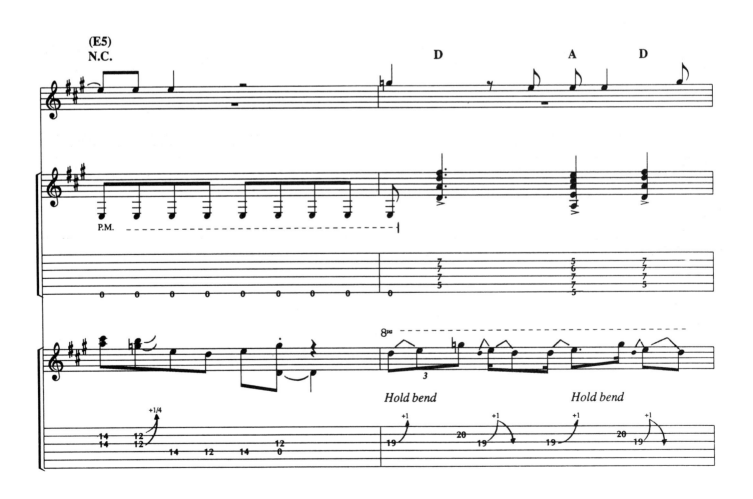

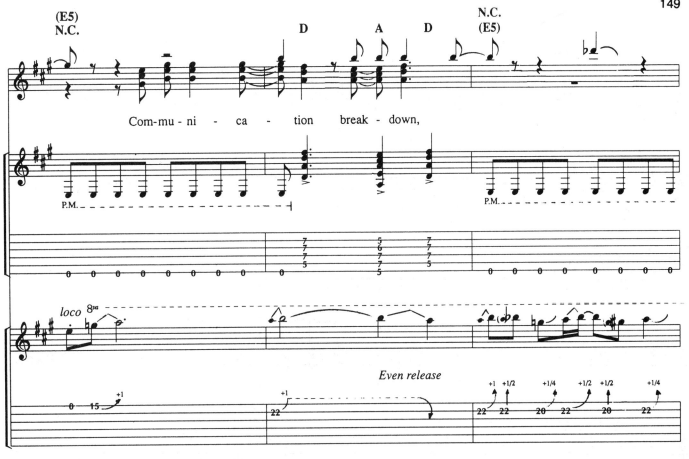

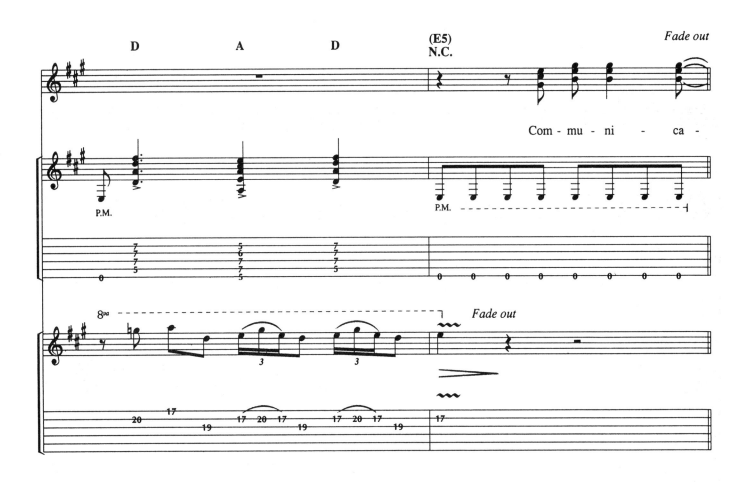

Black Dog

Words and Music by
JIMMY PAGE, ROBERT PLANT
and JOHN PAUL JONES

*Guitar 1 (Right channel) is in downstems and Guitar 2 (Left channel) is in upstems.

**This pitch is from a tape effect and not playable. See Performance Notes.

***Enter on drummer's cue.

****Guitar 2 enters and sustains its A5 chord into Verse 2, whereas
    Guitar 1 plays it's A5 chord again on the downbeat of Verse 2.

© 1972, 1992 SUPERHYPE PUBLISHING
All rights administered by WB MUSIC CORP.
All Rights Reserved

B C *Verses 2 and 3:*

Unh, nh child,_____ way you shake that thing,_____ gon - na
Heh, hey ba - by when you walk that way,_____ watch

Guitar 1 is faded out in the first measure. (Simile for all verses)

make you burn,_____ gon - na make you sting._____
heart - ache drip,_____ can't keep a - way._____

Guitars 1 and 2 **

**Guitar 2 joins Guitar 1 through Verse 3.*

D

*The Guitar 2 part omits the upper note of each power chord throughout the Chorus

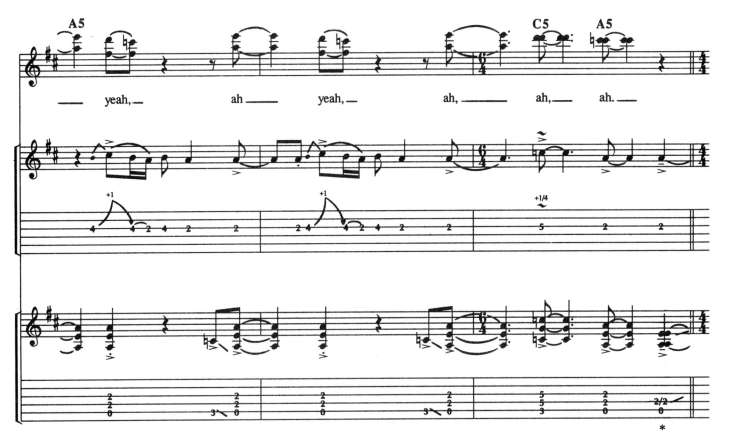

*Guitar 1 begins a slide up to A, while Guitar 2 repeats A5.

F **Verse 4:**

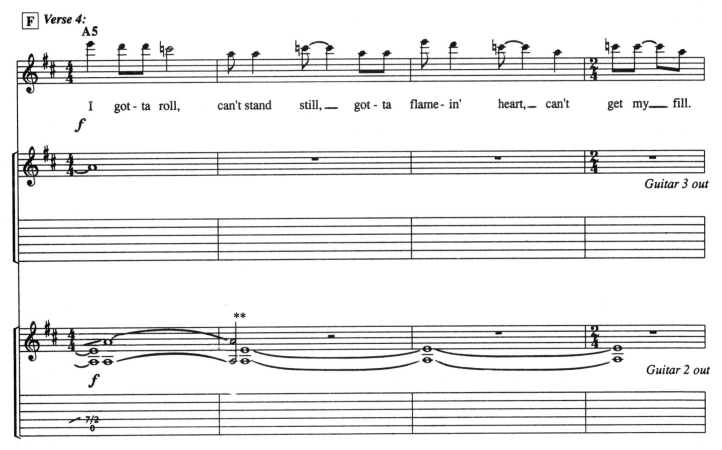

I got-ta roll, can't stand still, __ got-ta flame-in' heart, can't get my__ fill.

Guitar 3 out

Guitar 2 out

**Guitar 1 fades out and Guitar 2 sustains.

154

*Guitar 1 is faded out in the second measure.

**Guitar 1 is faded out in the second measure.

***Feedback harmonic

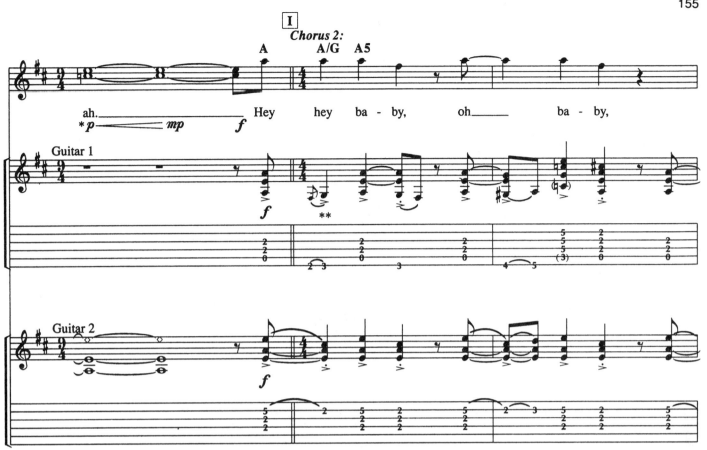

*Crescendo on upper note in vocal(e).
**Hammer on between thumb and second finger.

***Although these are the proper chords, various notes are emphasized each time they're strummed.
****The note E is played here by the Bass guitar only, throughout Choruses 2 and 3.

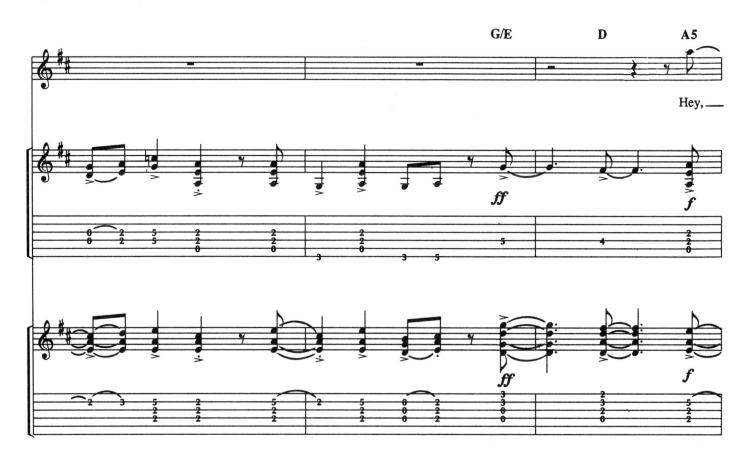

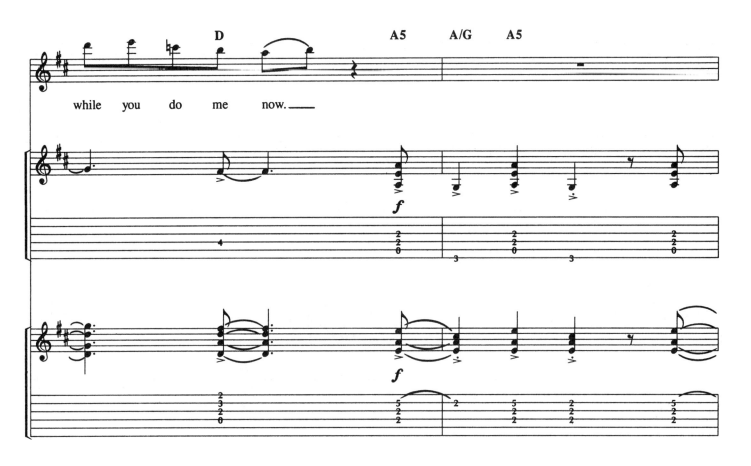

while you do me now.____

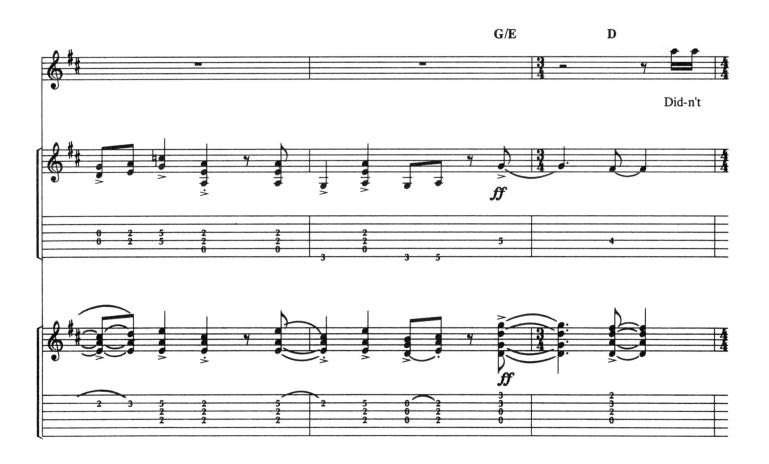

Did-n't

Guitar 1 fades out in measure 3.

*Guitar 1 fades out in measure 2.

Verse 8:

I don't know, ___ but I been told, ___ a big legged wom-an ___ ain't

got no soul. ___

be a star. _____

*The Guitar 1 and 2 parts have been combined.
The Guitar 2 part omits the upper note of each power chord throughout the Chorus.

All I ask ___ for, all I pray, ___ stead - y load - ed wom - an gon -

Guitar 1 slides into A5 and fades out in measure 2, Guitar 2 sustains.

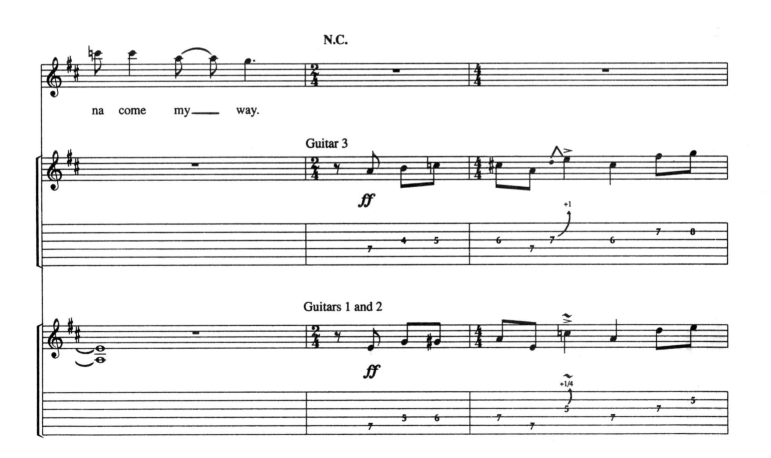

na come my ___ way.

N.C.

Guitar 3

Guitars 1 and 2

A5

P *Verse 10:*

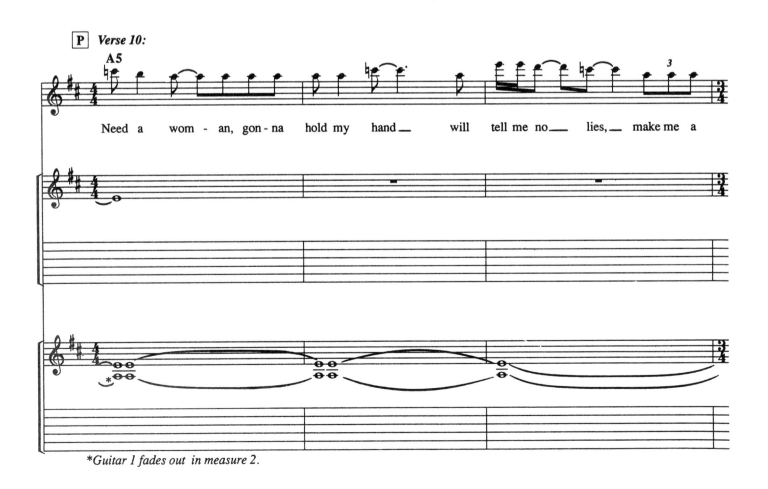

Need a wom - an, gon - na hold my hand__ will tell me no__ lies,__ make me a

*Guitar 1 fades out in measure 2.

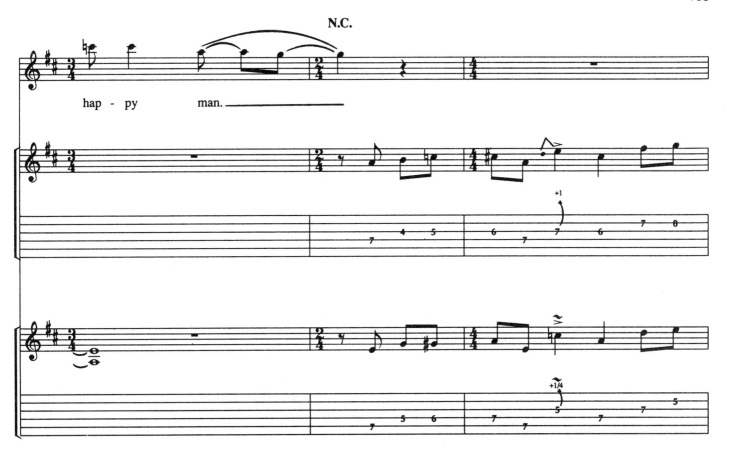

hap - py man._____

Q Bridge:

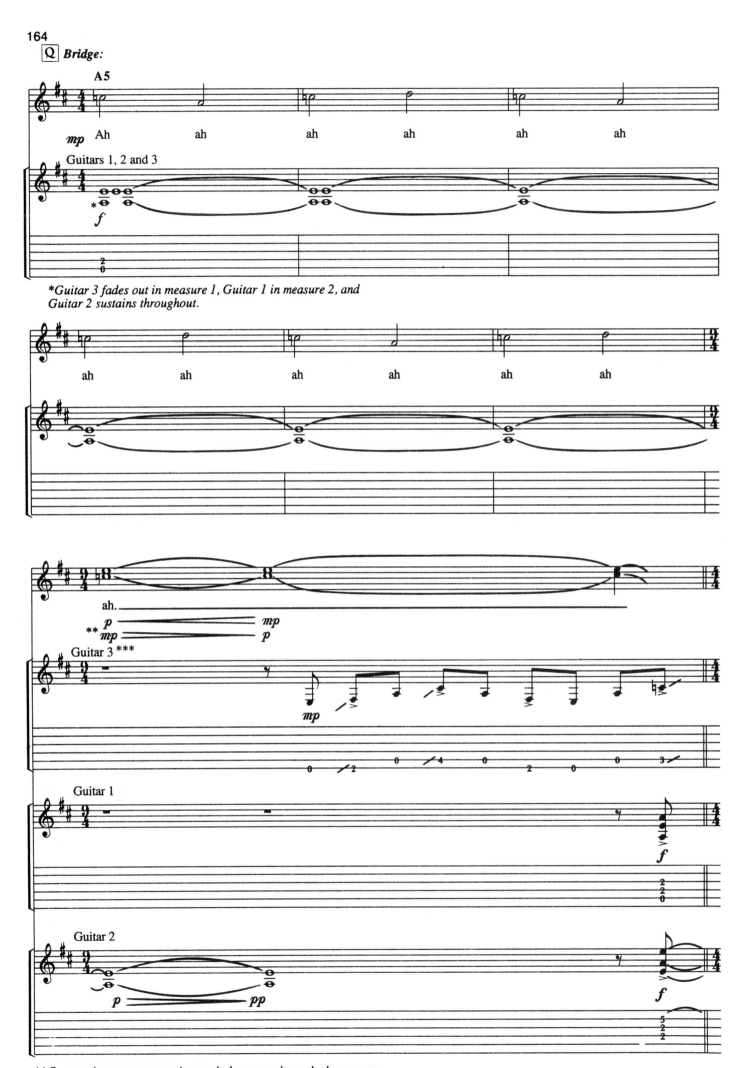

*Guitar 3 fades out in measure 1, Guitar 1 in measure 2, and
Guitar 2 sustains throughout.

**Crescendo on upper note in vocal, decrescendo on the lower note.
***Guitar 3 is recorded through a Leslie amplifier (rotating speakers), and on a separate track with a standard amplifier.

R

Chorus 3(Guitar solo):

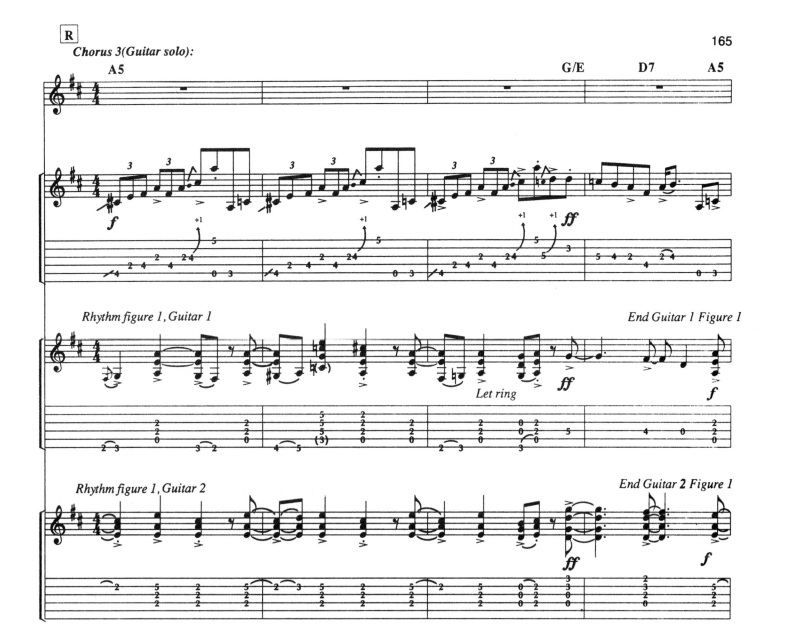

*Standard amplifier from here on, no Leslie.
**Volume in mix is much lower.

166

167

Push it, ba-by, push it, ba-by, push it, ba-by,

push it, ba-by, push it, ba-by, push it, babe

babe.

*Leslie amp returns, standard amp out.

Begin Guitar 4 figure 2
Guitar 4**

End Guitar 4 figure 2

Guitar 3

**Continue with Guitar 2, figure 1.*

**Guitar 1, figure 1 mixed lower to make room for Guitar 4, figure 1. (Right Channel)*

Continue figure 1, Guitars 1 and 2 and continue figure 2, Guitar 4, 6 times till fade.

Heartbreaker

Words and Music by
JIMMY PAGE, ROBERT PLANT,
JOHN PAUL JONES and JOHN BONHAM

Hey, fel-las have you heard the news,__ you know that An-nie's back__ in town.__ It

won't take long till some-one can see all the fel-las lay their mo-ney down? Her

© 1969, 1990 SUPERHYPE PUBLISHING
All rights administered by WB MUSIC CORP.
All Rights Reserved

style is new___ but the face's the same___ as it was so long a - go, but

from her eyes___ a dif-'frent smile___ like that of one who?___ knows.___

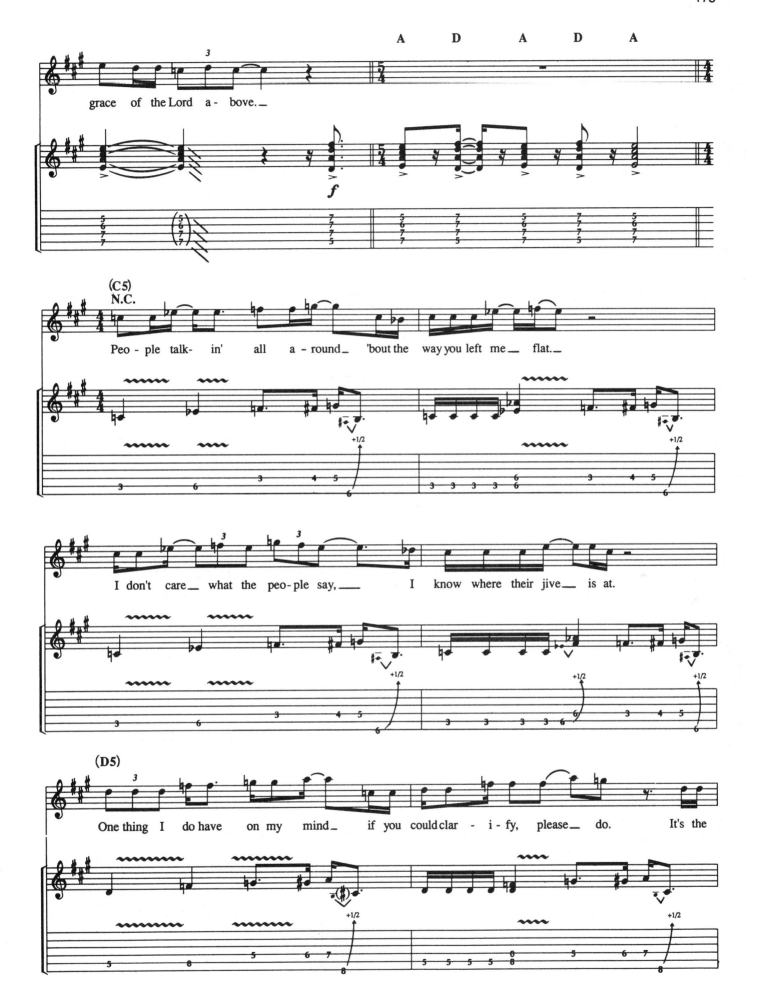

* Accidentals apply only to indicated notes throughout freetime solo.

** Bend strings behind nut.

Bron-Y-Aur Stomp

Moderate Country Folk Dance ♩ = 116
Intro:
Acoustic Guitar* (open F tuning)

Words and Music by
JIMMY PAGE, ROBERT PLANT
and JOHN PAUL JONES

*Tuning: ⑥ D, ⑤ A, ④ D, ③ F#, ② A, ① D; capoed at 3.
All fret numbers are counted from the nut, not the capo (3=open).*

**Harmonics: Tilt hand and lightly touch strings with fourth finger at XV.*

****Feel it like 4/8 + 2/4; double time: "1-2-3-4" and regular time: "1-2," for four measures, begining with measure 3, beat 3.
Also, bar all six strings for all chords, but primarily strum only those strings indicated.*

© 1970, 1991 SUPERHYPE PUBLISHING
All rights administered by WB MUSIC CORP.
All Rights Reserved

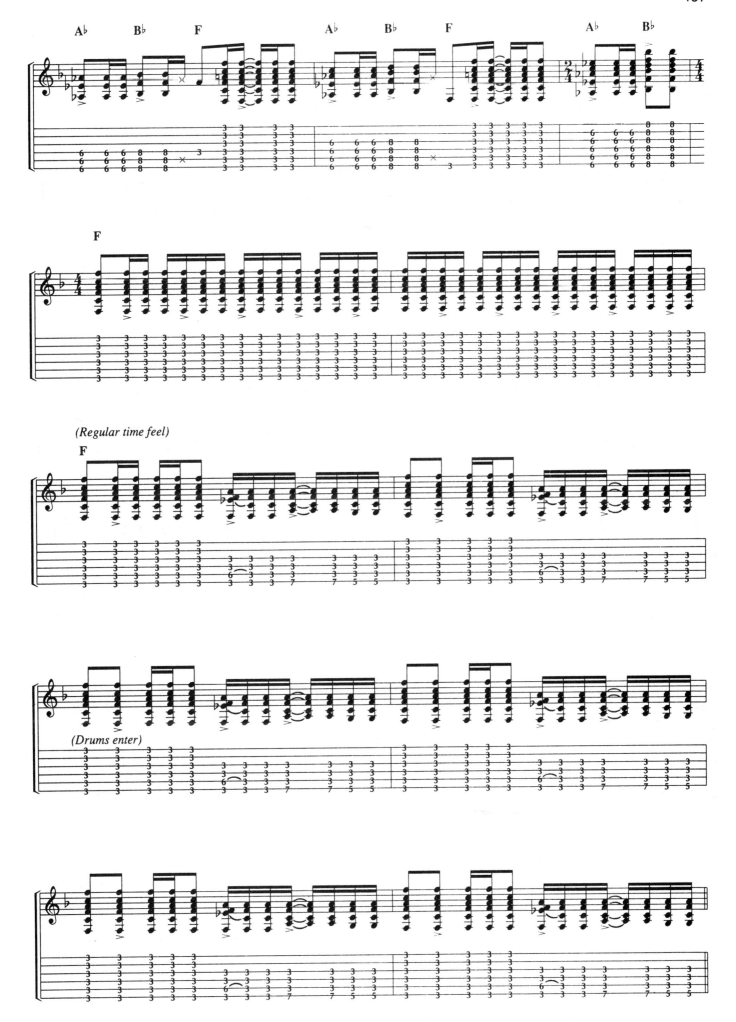

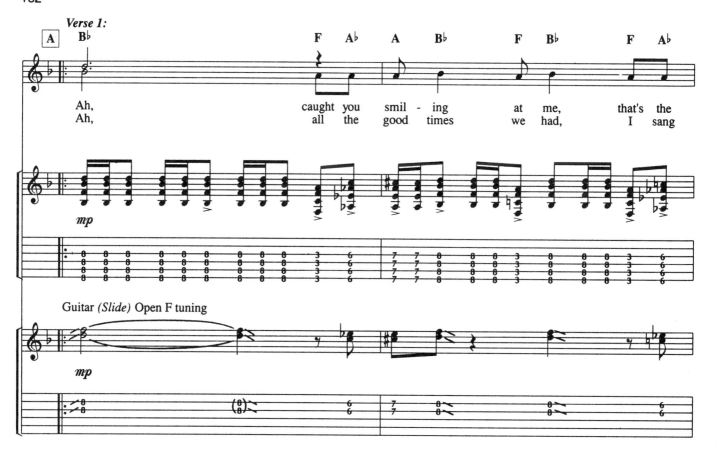

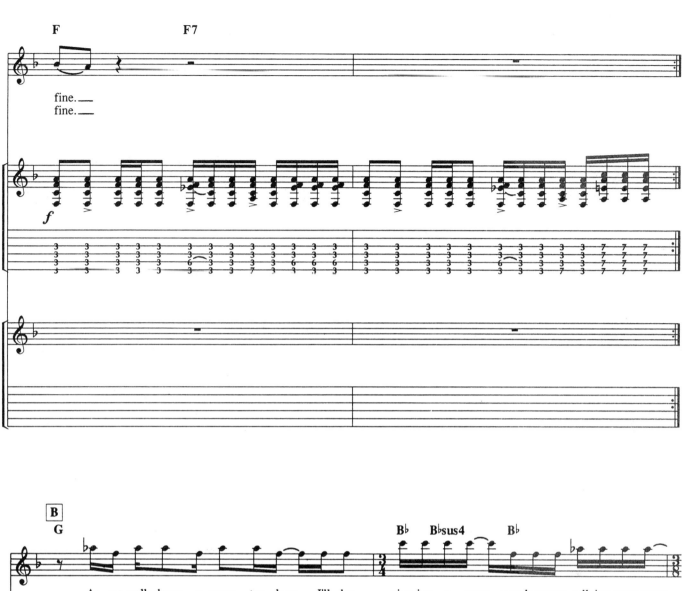

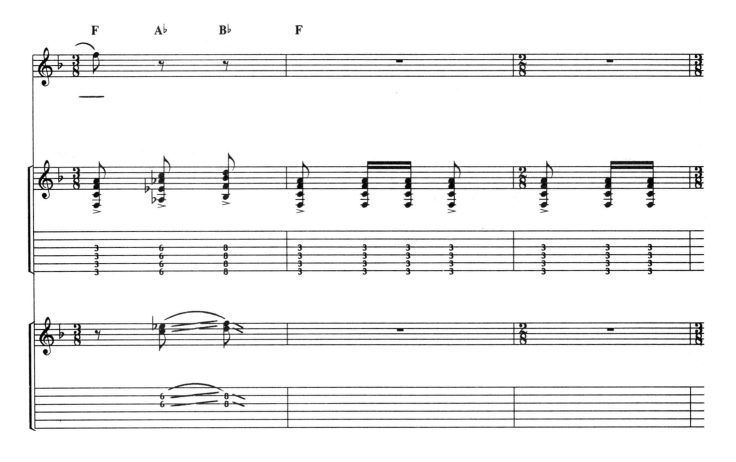

Hear the wind whis-per in the trees __ tell-ing Moth-er Na - ture 'bout you and me.

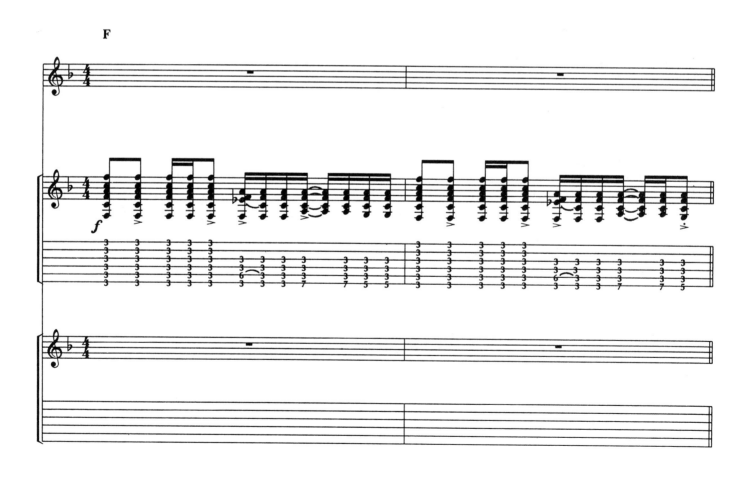

Lower part is lead vocal throughout.

Verse 3:

Ah, can a love be so strong when so man-y loves go wrong? Will our

love go on and on, and on, and on, and on, and on?

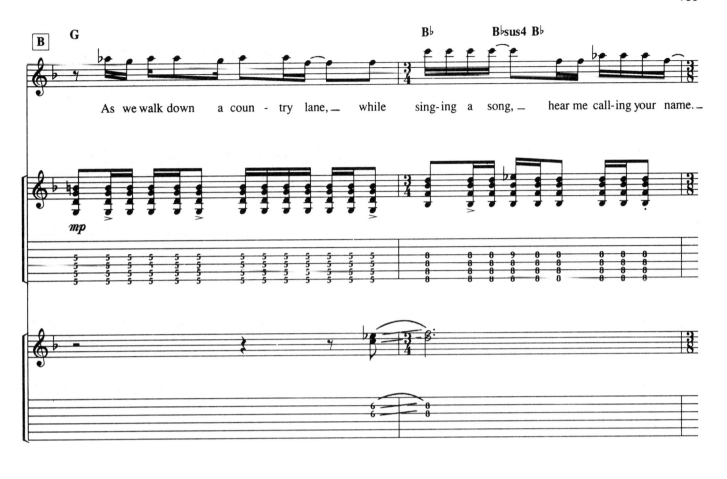

As we walk down a coun - try lane, — while sing-ing a song, — hear me call-ing your name. —

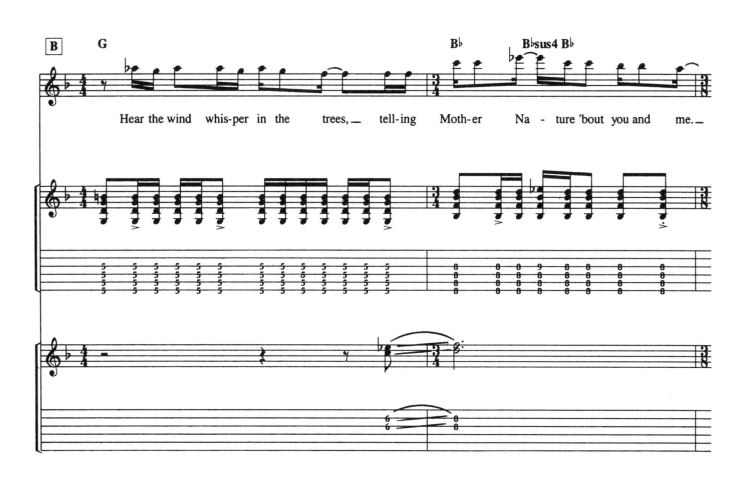

Hear the wind whis-per in the trees,__ tell-ing Moth-er Na - ture 'bout you and me.__

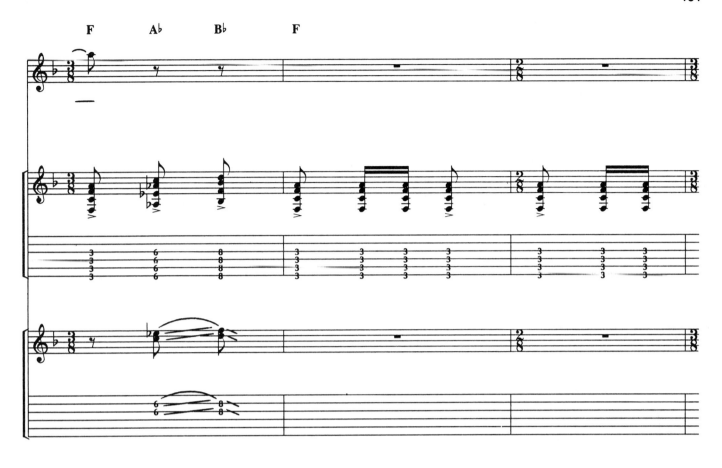

192

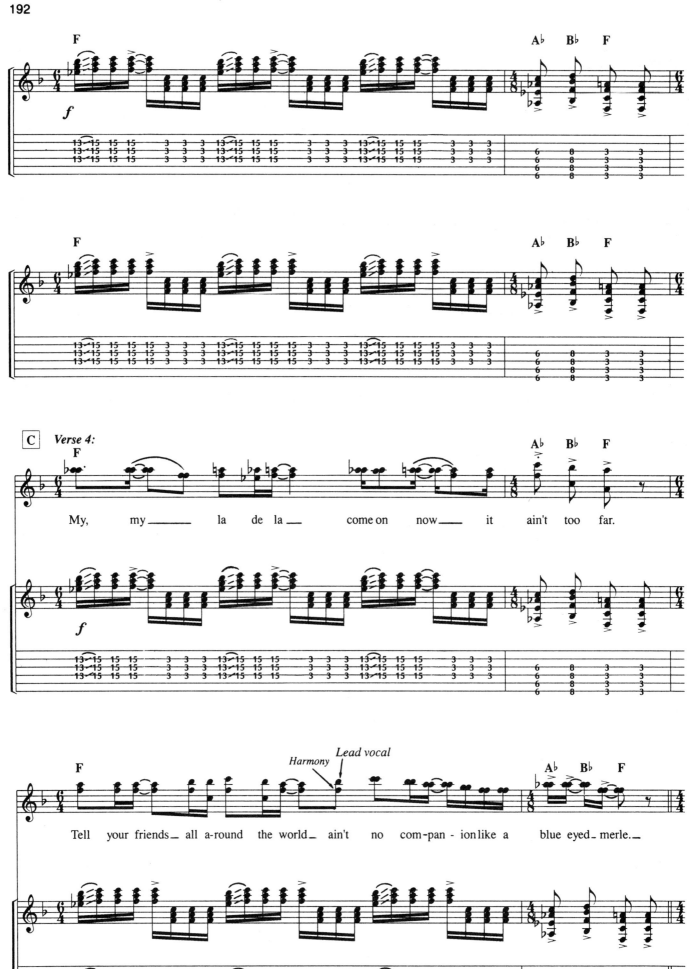

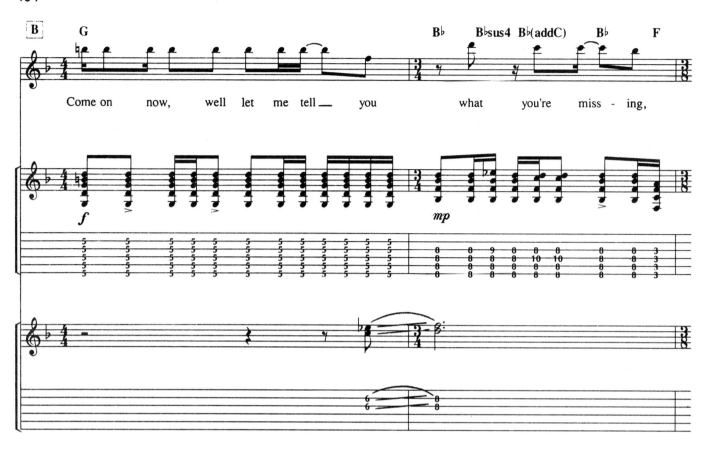

Come on now, well let me tell__ you what you're miss - ing,

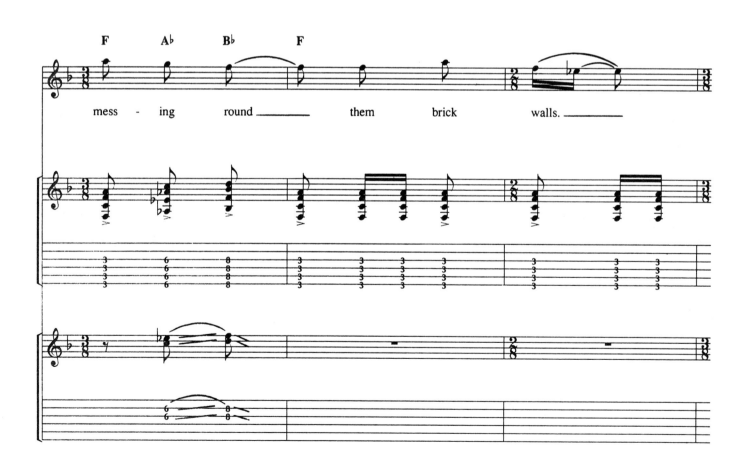

mess - ing round _____ them brick walls. _____

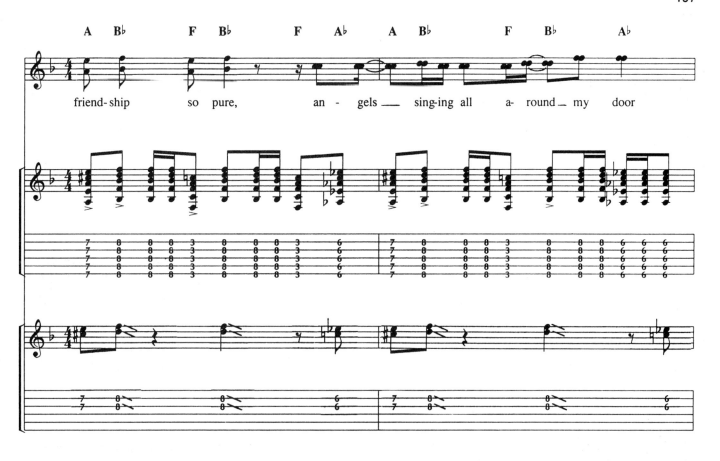

friend-ship   so   pure,   an - gels ___ sing-ing all   a- round ___ my   door

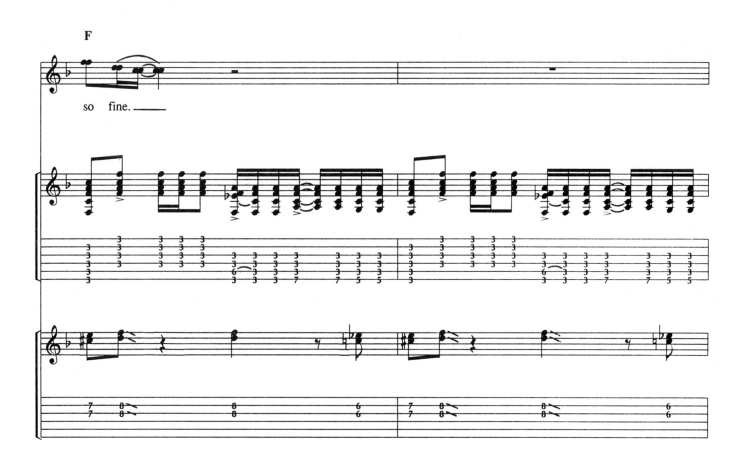

so   fine. _____

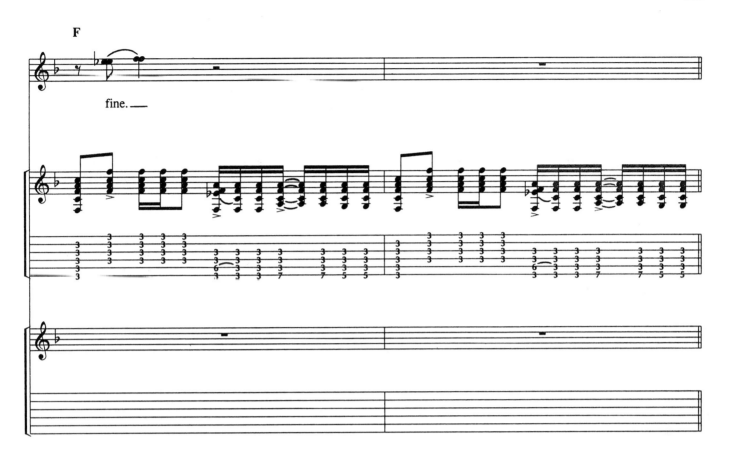

F

fine.___

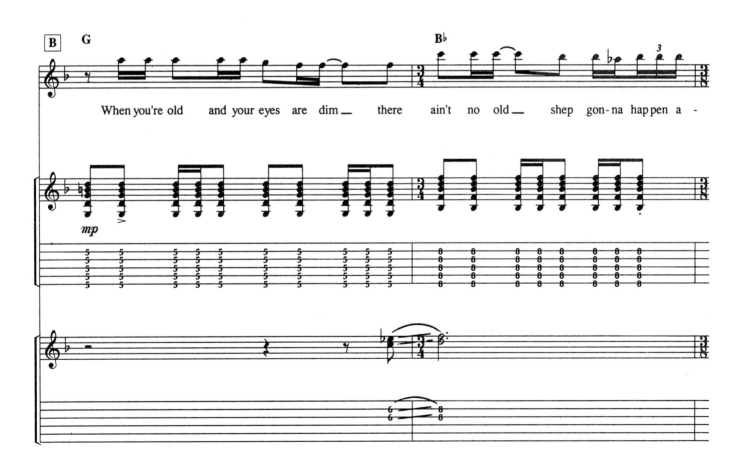

B **G**

When you're old   and your eyes are dim___ there   ain't no old___ shep gon-na hap pen a -

mp

gain.

We'll still go walk-ing down coun - try

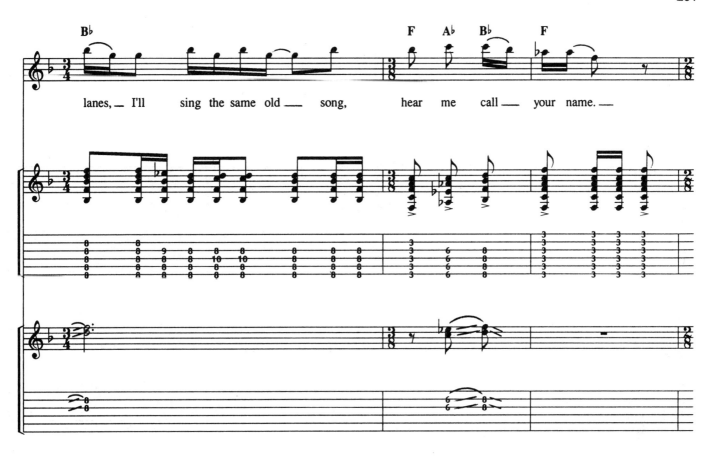

lanes, __ I'll   sing the same old __ song,   hear me call __ your name. __

Going To California

Words and Music by
JIMMY PAGE and
ROBERT PLANT

Country Folk Ballad Slowly ♩ = 78

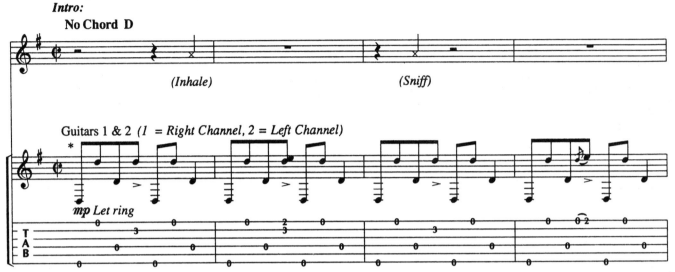

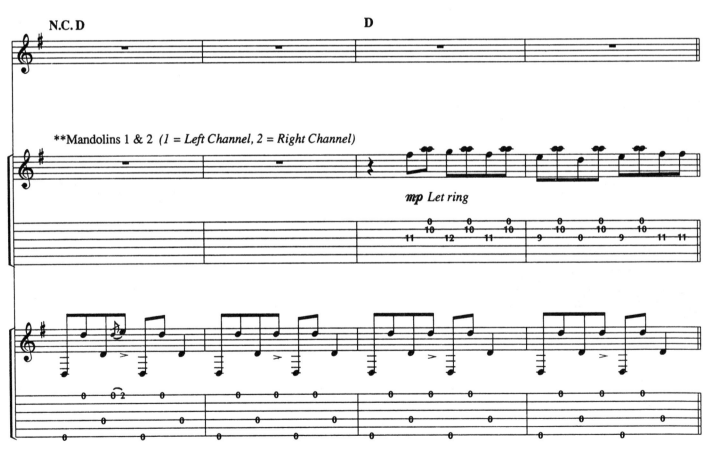

*Tuning: ⑥ = D, ⑤ = A, ④ = D, ③ = G, ② = B, ① = D.

**Both Mandolins are arranged for Guitars in the above tuning that are capoed at VII.
All notes at VII are notated as open in the TAB.

© 1972, 1992 SUPERHYPE PUBLISHING
All rights administered by WB MUSIC CORP.
All Rights Reserved

*Suggested fingering: ⑥ = second finger, ① = third finger.

drank,   all   my   wine.___

*Notes in parenthesis may be an overdubbed jaw harp, or EQ effect.

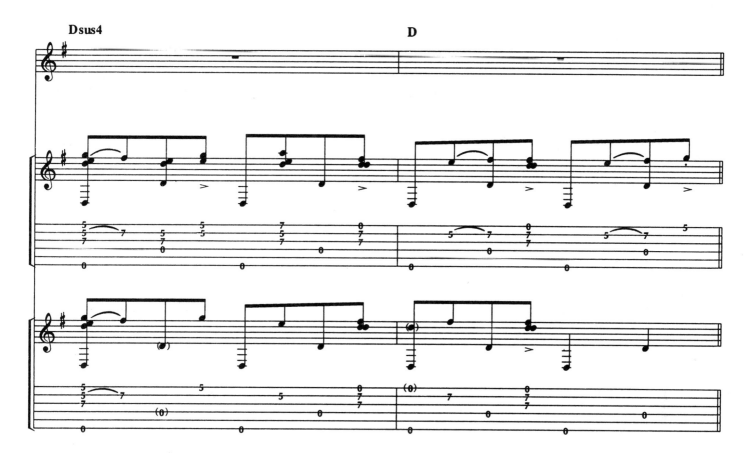

C *Verse:*

With Mandolins 1 & 2 Figures 1

Some-one told___ me there's a   girl out   there,___   with love in her eyes,___   and

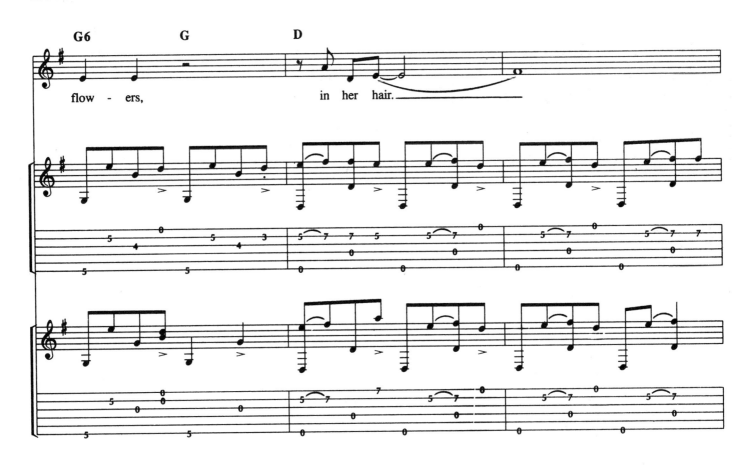

flow - ers,   in her hair.

End Guitar 1 Figure 1

E *Verse:*

With Mandolin 2 Figure 1 & Guitar 1 Figure 1

Took my chances___ on a big jet plane,___ nev - er let them tell ya' that they're

Mandolin 1

Guitar 2

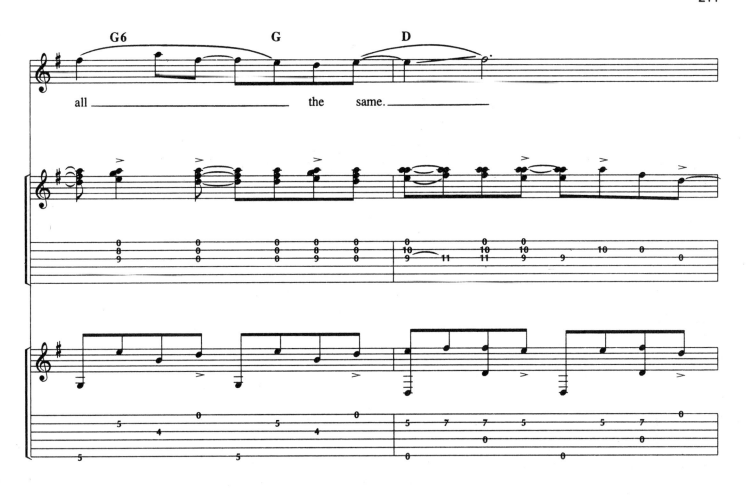

all _____ the same. _____

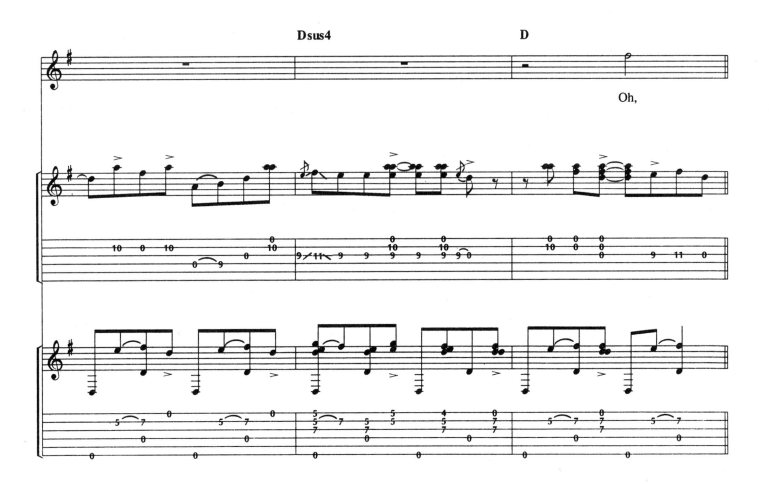

Oh,

F *Verse:*
With Mandolin 2 Figure 1 & Guitar 1 Figure 1

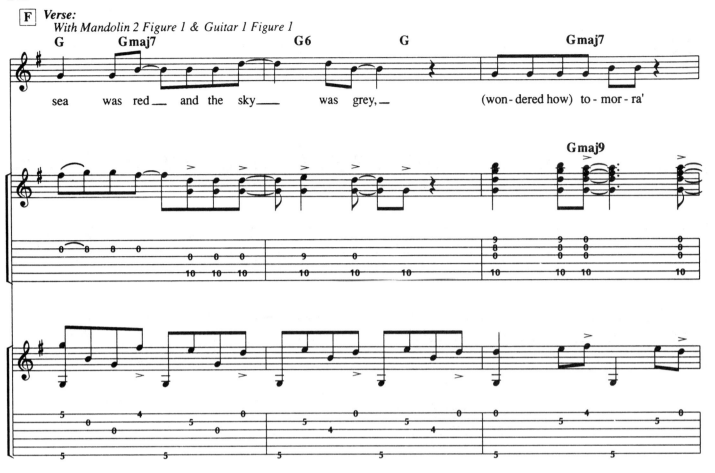

sea was red __ and the sky __ was grey, __ (won-dered how) to-mor-ra'

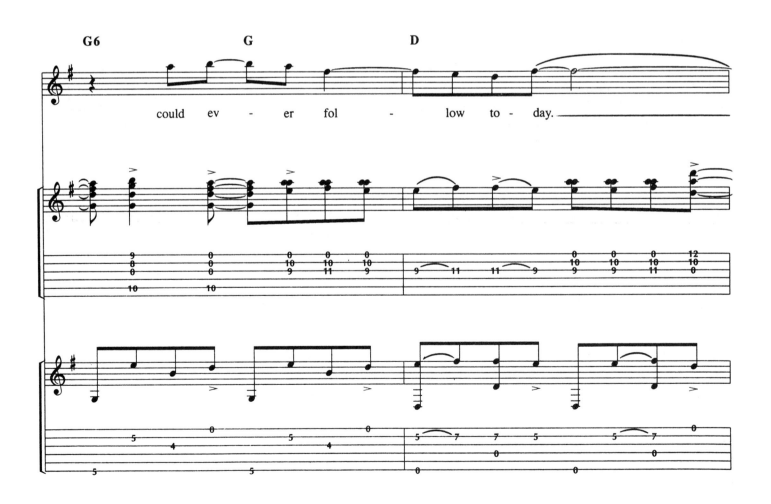

could ev - er fol - low to - day. __

G Verse:
With Mandolin 2 Figure 1 & Guitar 1 Figure 1

Moun- tains and the can- yons start to trem- ble and shake,__ child-ren of the sun be - gin__

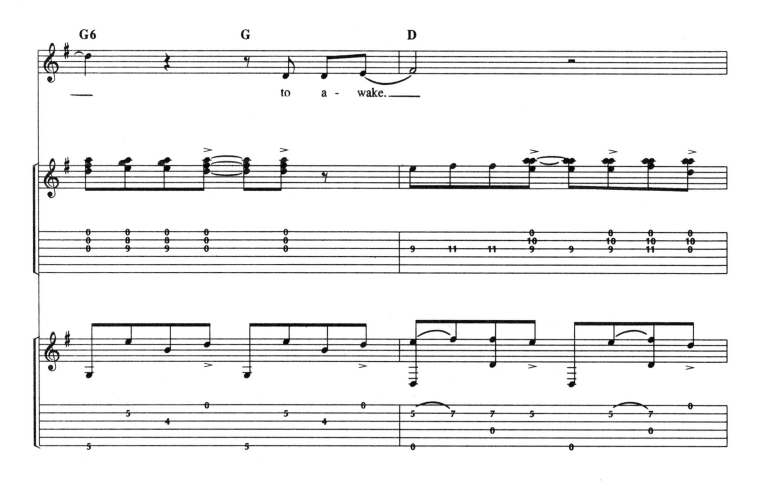

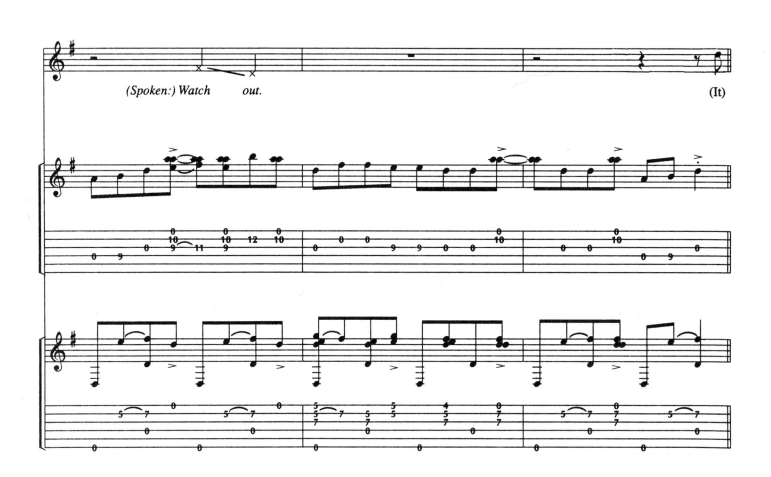

*Strummed with the thumb instead of finger picked.
Notes in parentheses appear on one track only and may be omitted when impractical.

J Verse:
With Mandolin 1 Figure 1
and Mandolin 2 Figure 1

To find a queen ___ with-out ___

___ a king, they say she plays ___ gui-tar ___ and cries ___ and

sings. ____ La, la, la, la.

End Guitar 2 Figure 2

K **Verse:**
With Mandolin 1 & 2 Figures 1 and Guitar 2 Figure 2 (2 times) w/ ad lib variations

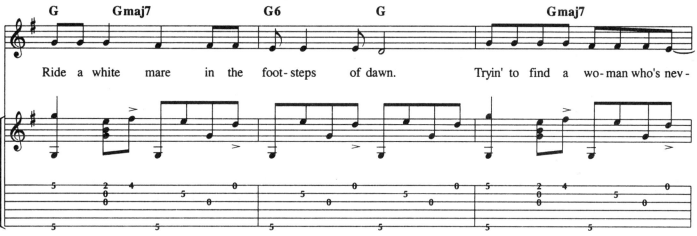

Ride a white mare in the foot-steps of dawn. Tryin' to find a wo-man who's nev-

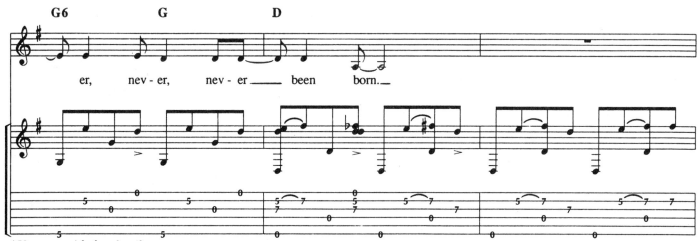

er, nev-er, nev-er ____ been born. ____

*Upstrum with thumbnail.
**Upstrum with pad of finger.

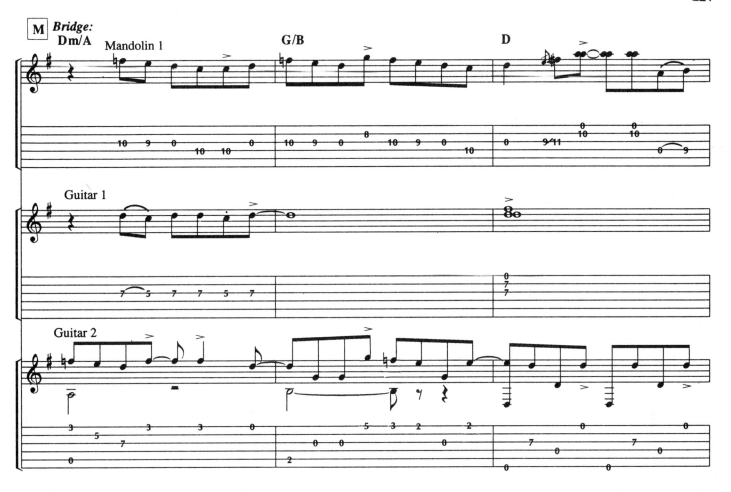

D

N **Outro:**
With Guitar 1 Figure 3 (to fade)

Guitar 3

*Jaw Harp through reverse echo return.

Figure 3
Guitar 1

Misty Mountain Hop

Words and Music by
JIMMY PAGE, ROBERT PLANT
and JOHN PAUL JONES

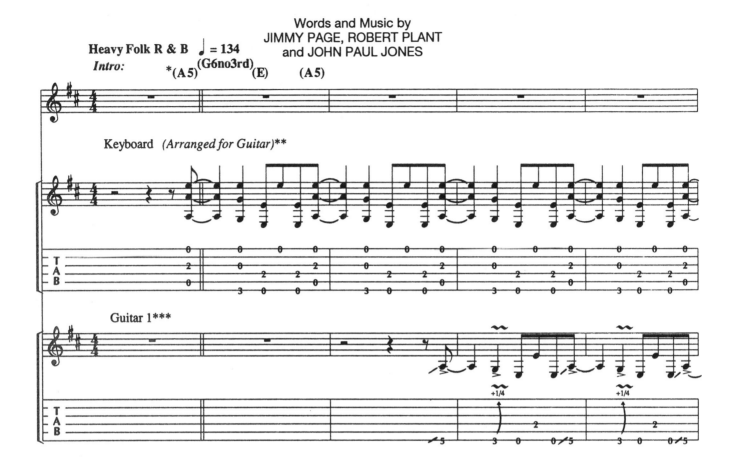

All chords in parentheses are implied. Pattern continues throughout main riff.

**Electric piano (Wurlitzer type) part arranged for a second guitar. (Left channel)
This figure is repeated throughout the Intro and whenever the actual Guitar 1 part appears.

***The actual Guitar 1 part. (Right channel). Treble pick-up with distortion.*

© 1972, 1992 SUPERHYPE PUBLISHING
All rights administered by WB MUSIC CORP.
All Rights Reserved

*Chord names for reference only. Pattern continues until restatement of main riff.

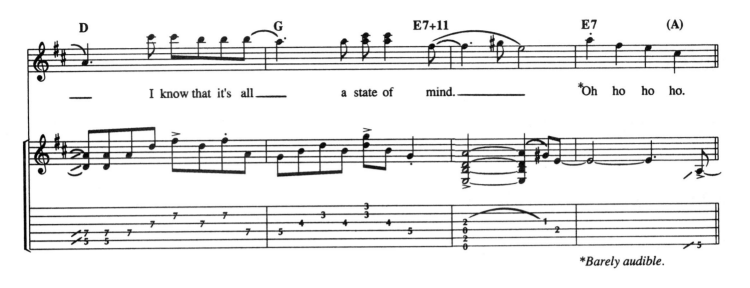

I know that it's all____ a state of mind._____ *Oh ho ho ho.

*Barely audible.

G **Bridge:** *(Guitar Solo)*

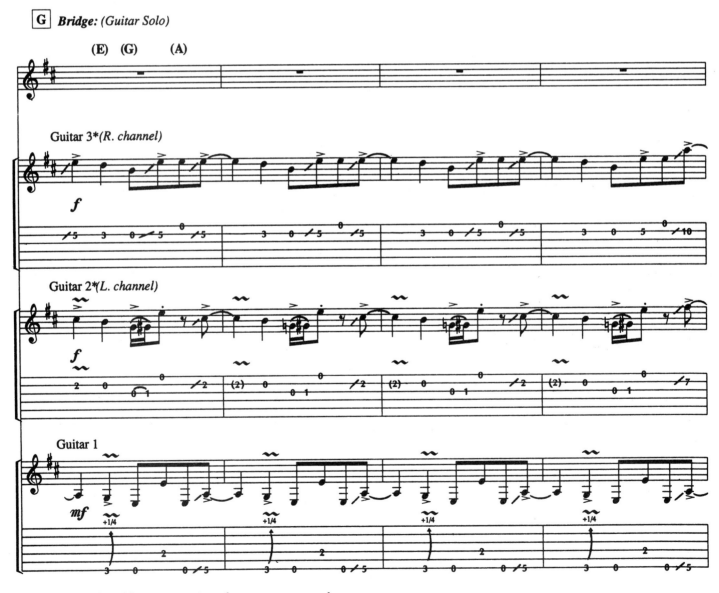

Guitar parts 2 and 3 are composites of many separate tracks.

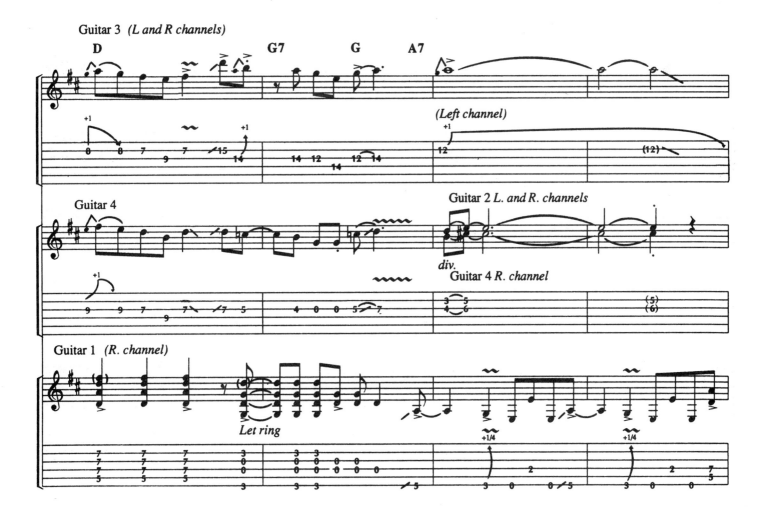

What Is And What Should Never Be

Words and Music by
JIMMY PAGE and
ROBERT PLANT

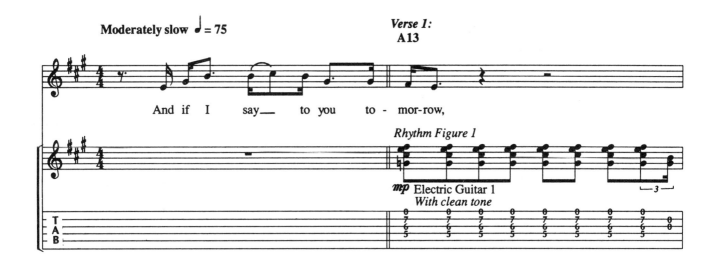

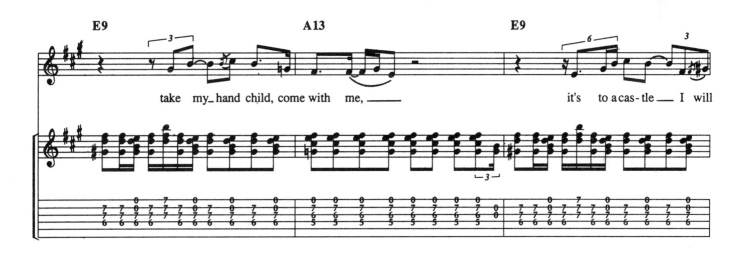

© 1969, 1990 SUPERHYPE PUBLISHING
All rights administered by WB MUSIC CORP.
All Rights Reserved

* Third string rings sympathetically

243

Friends

Words and Music by
JIMMY PAGE and
ROBERT PLANT

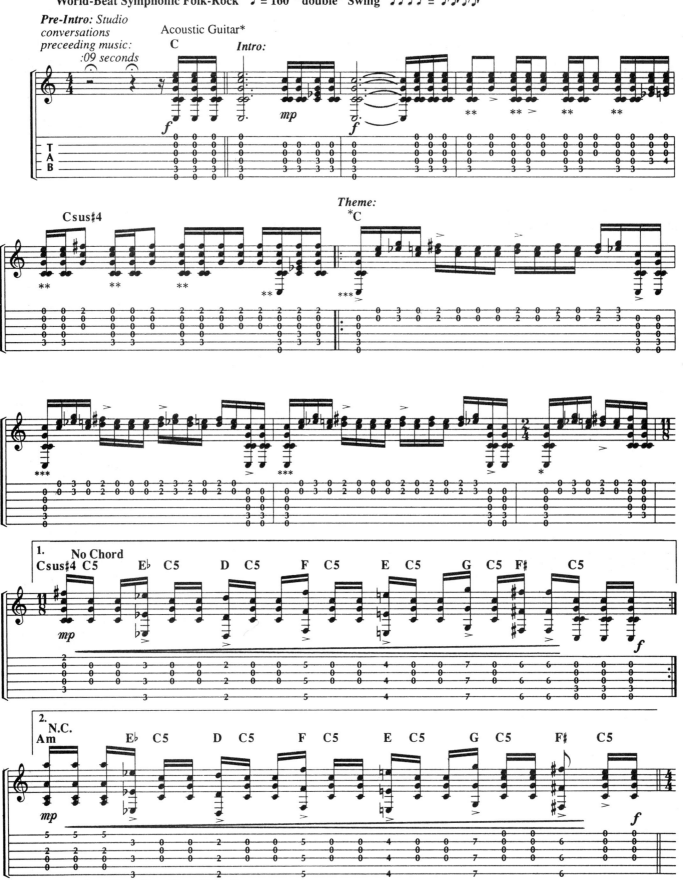

*C tuning: ⑥C, ⑤A, ④C, ③G, ②C, ①E.

**Let ring

***Chords alternate between C5, C minor, and Csus9/#11.

© 1970, 1991 SUPERHYPE PUBLISHING
All rights administered by WB MUSIC CORP.
All Rights Reserved

Verse 1:

Let ring. Double-time "swing" feel throughout section.
**Continue with varied accent intensity on all upbeats throughout Verse and Chorus.*

*Let ring.

*Quickly hammer fingers on to ⑥ and ④ (muting ⑤) and begin slide up to VII.

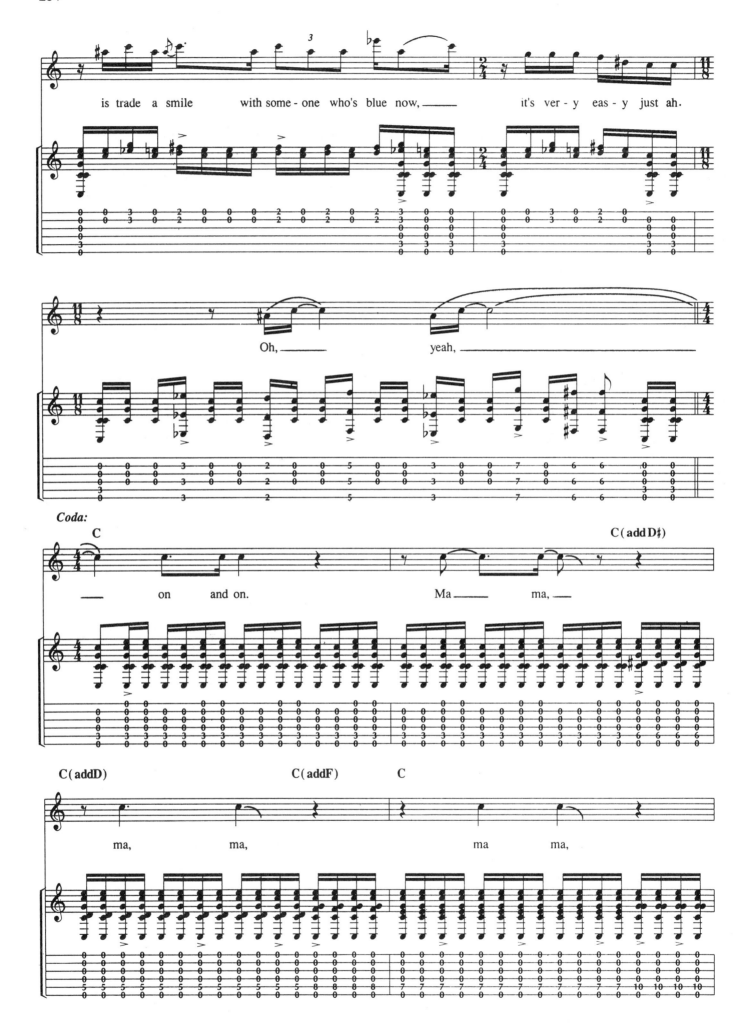

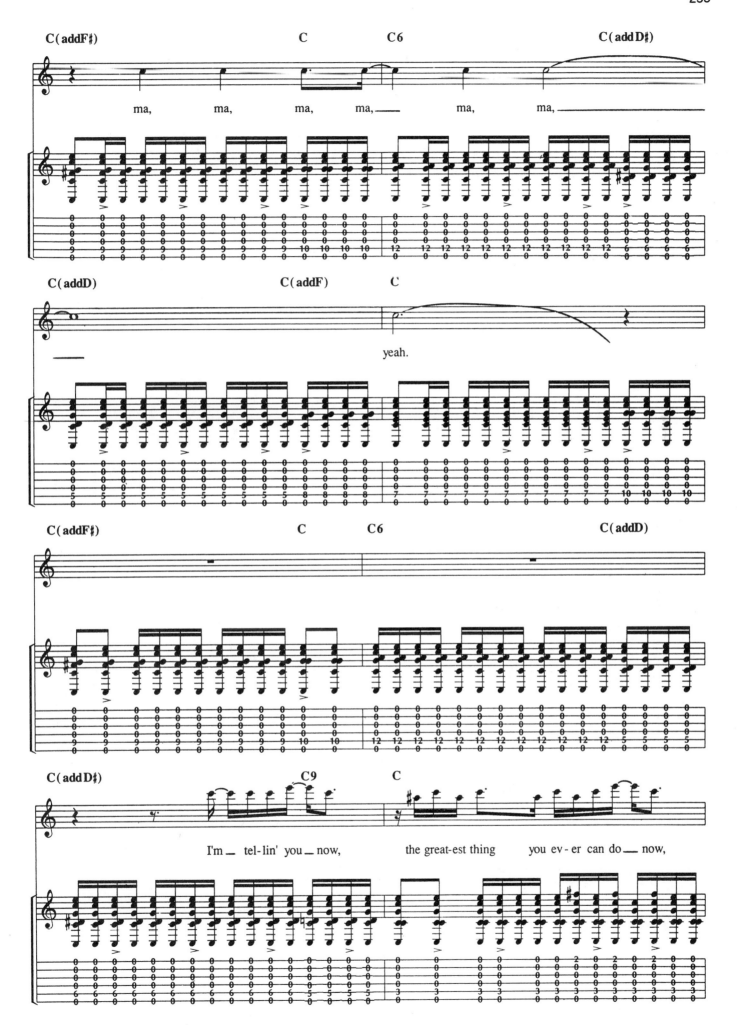

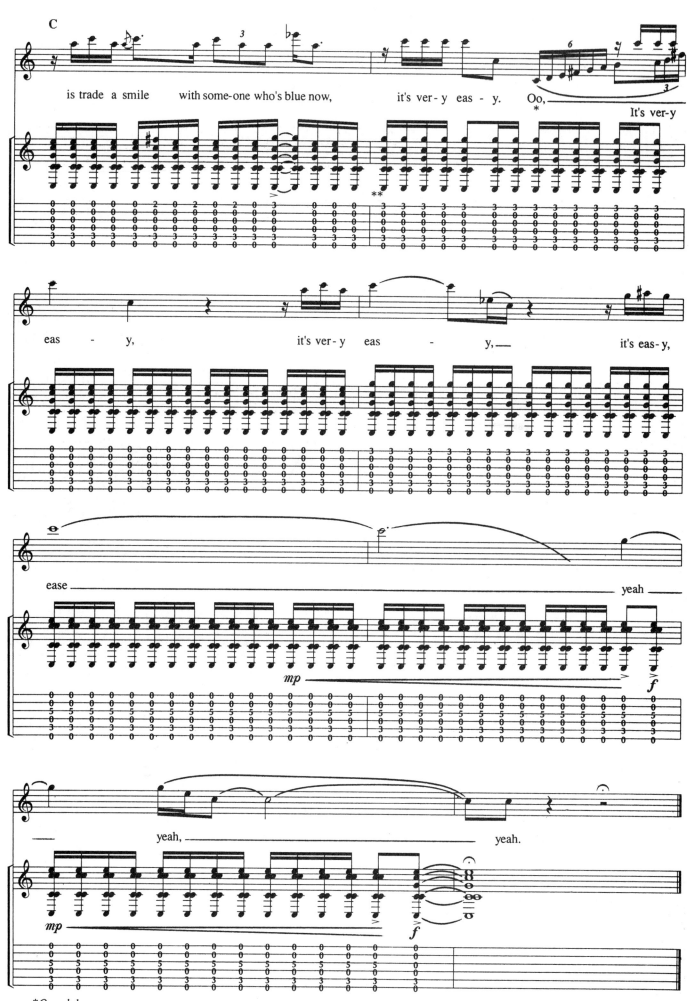

is trade a smile   with some-one who's blue now,   it's ver-y eas - y.   Oo, _____
It's ver-y

eas - y,   it's ver-y eas   - y, ____   it's eas-y,

ease _____ yeah _____

_____ yeah, _____ yeah.

*Overdub.
**Emphasize ⑥-③ from here on.